July 22/82.

Marty:-

Do hope you enjoy this book.

9984

The NEW Book of
MOTORCYCLES

Erik Arctander

New York

Published by ARCO PUBLISHING COMPANY, Inc.
219 Park Avenue South, New York, N.Y. 10003

Fifth Printing, 1974

Copyright © Fawcett Publications, Inc., 1968
All Rights Reserved

Library of Congress Catalog Number 68-54470

ISBN 0-668-01813-5

Printed in U.S.A.

About the Author

Erik H. Arctander, author of this book, began motorcycling almost by accident, in 1948, at the ripe age of 25. A student at Columbia College back from four years as a deck officer in the merchant marine, he needed inexpensive transportation to visit relatives in Scandinavia. Distances were too great for a bicycle, so he picked up a new 125 cc Excelsior two-stroke in England and took it by North Sea steamer to Denmark.

Without registration or driver's license he was forced to take motorcycle riding lessons in a school.

His mount was a pre-WW II BSA with four-speed hand shift. Everyone else rode Denmark's four-cylinder Nimbus, since extinct. After a week's intensive practice in driving, motorcycle theory and driving rules he passed his test in the busiest square in Copenhagen.

The author sold the Excelsior in Oslo, Norway to a divinity student for plane fare home. Bitten badly by the motorcycle bug, he bought a second-hand 1946 Indian Chief six months later. Soon after, he met his future wife in a motorcycle shop—she owned a 350 cc Panther. Since then it has been a motorcycle family. In 1950, as a young couple, they began watching and then competing in Sunday club events.

Soon both were writing articles and taking photos for *Motorcyclist,* a California magazine. A writer and editor by profession, the author gradually extended his free-lancing to other magazines, as well. Despite motorcycling's rapid acceptance in recent years, for him it has remained a hobby. His full-time job? Associate director of publications for the College Entrance Examination Board.

CONTENTS

A Treasury of American Motorcycles

By Emmett Moore

(Emmett Moore is a veteran motorcyclist and a founder of the Antique Motorcycle Club of America. Formerly with the Indian Motorcycle Co. and BSA Eastern, he is now Dealer Services Manager for Eastern Kawasaki Motorcycle Corp.)

SIXTY-SIX years have now elapsed since the first motorcycles were commercially produced in America—years filled with a tremendous number of makes and a wealth of original thinking in motorcycle design. Unfortunately, all of these enterprises, save one, have died. Some lived briefly, some flourished for long years; all have left a heritage that is remembered by a comparatively small group of enthusiasts, among them members of the Antique Motorcycle Club of America.

Author's son straddles 1930 Indian Scout, called the "101" because it could go 101 mph. With girder forks and leaf-spring suspension, no rear shocks, it's a hard rider. But carnival riders still use them.

INDIAN 101 SCOUT
(specifications)

Engine type:
Four-stroke, side-valve vee-twin
Displacement: 750 cc (45 cu. in.) or
600 cc (37 cu. in.)
Bore/stroke: 2⅞ in. x 3½ in.
Horsepower: 20 (est.)   Speeds: 3
Ignition: Magneto   Miles/gallon: 50
Top speed: 70-75   Weight: 365 lbs.
Tires: 3.85x18 clincher. 1930 and later,
4.00x18 drop-center

1929 Harley-Davidson (above and right) pulled a sidecar. Hand shift, foot clutch were on left side. Tank under the horn held acetylene gas to fuel two headlights.

From this vast storehouse of memorable makes, it is extremely difficult for the buff to choose a few favorites. Inevitably the choice will be a personal one, but here are mine.

The Indian 101 Scout

First in my thoughts, because it was my first motorcycle, this famous model is also considered a classic by many of those associated with antique and vintage motorcycle clubs around the world. Some believe it to be the best motorcycle ever built in America. With some reservations, I share that thought. The 101 is a masterpiece, though with some faults.

The original Indian Scout was designed by Charles Franklin, an ex-British racing star and engineer who came to the big motorcycle factory in Springfield, Mass., before 1920. He created the Scout series, which for some years was powered by a 37-cubic-inch (600 cc) side-valve engine with extremely reliable but rather meek characteristics. In 1927, a much more potent 45-cubic-inch (750 cc) engine made its appearance; but the machine, although successful, still suffered from a frumpy appearance. During 1928, Franklin went to work on a redesign, and late in the year, the 101 made its first appearance (as a 1929 model). It was an immediate sensation.

Even to modern eyes, the design of the 101 looks "right." The lines of the frame and tank give it a light, graceful appear-

> **1929 HARLEY-DAVIDSON 74**
> **(specifications)**
>
> **Engine type:**
> **Four-stroke, F-head vee-twin**
> **Displacement: 1,207 cc (74 cu. in.)**
> **Bore/stroke: (not available)**
> **Horsepower: 35 (est.)**
> **Ignition: Battery and coil**
> **Top speed: 85-90**
> **Speeds: 3**
> **Miles/gallon: 35-40**
> **Weight: 450 lbs. (est.)**
> **Tires: 3.85x19 clincher front and rear**

ance, and the compact semi-unit power plant is notable for an absence of clutter. All possible wiring, control cables, and oil lines are concealed, and the complete machine is much cleaner in appearance than many of today's makes. Best of all, this remarkable motorcycle possesses an exceptional degree of stability and handles to perfection. So good are its manners, that to this very day a 101 is often the mainstay of the carnival rider who circles high up on the wooden wall of his "motordrome."

The frame is a very heavy double-loop type built up of tubing with malleable iron lugs. All joints are brazed. Front forks, of built-up type, incorporate a leaf-spring which controls a rather limited wheel movement. (Total movement is only about two inches.) The rear frame is rigid, and consequently the ride is quite hard. Even though the pan-type saddle is suspended on coil springs, the rider soon learned to get his weight up on the footboards when a bump was spotted. On a rough road, the 101 Scout could make even an ardent supporter unhappy. Indian had a slogan: "You can't wear out an Indian Scout." It was true—usually the rider wore out first.

The Indian Scout 45-cubic-inch engine was a marvel of simplicity, produced great power for its day, and was entirely reliable if not abused. I personally rode a 101 for eight consecutive years, in the late '30s and early '40s, without the engine ever failing me.

The cylinders are iron castings, as are the cylinder heads. Valves are side by side, 1¾ inches in diameter. Both main and big-end bearings are of the heavy-duty roller type. A mechanical pump provides oiling by the once-common total-loss system. Ignition is by Splitdorf magneto, with separate belt-driven generator for lights and horn. Transmission is three-speed, with

a direct-acting gearshift lever operated by the right hand. The clutch is a heavy multiple-disc, wet type. Primary drive is by helical-cut gears (which never wore out) and final drive is by chain. Transmission is bolted directly to the crankcase in semi-unit style, and the entire engine-transmission assembly can be removed from the frame in less than 30 minutes.

In the 45-cubic-inch version (a 37-incher was also available) the machine was fast for its day—too fast for the inadequate braking provided. The seven-inch front wheel internal-expanding brake is very weak, and the external-contracting rear-wheel brake is a relic inherited from much earlier Indian models. In 1931 (the last year the 101 was made) Indian fitted better internal-expanding brakes both front and rear.

Many Indian 101 Scouts have survived down to the present time, having inspired loyal ownership very early. I still take a short spin on my 1930 model—owned since new—taking care that the road selected is a smooth one!

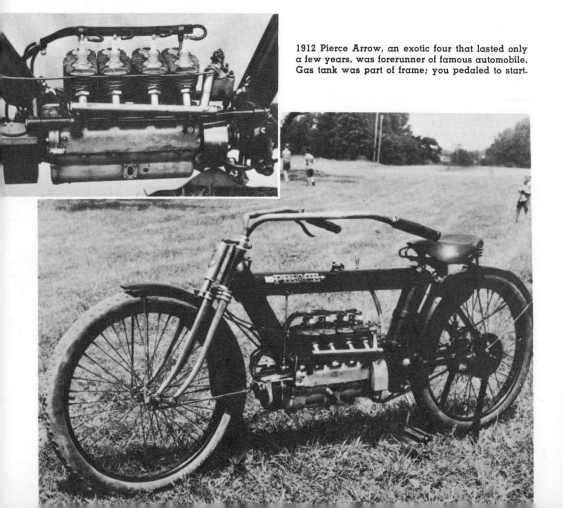

1912 Pierce Arrow, an exotic four that lasted only a few years, was forerunner of famous automobile. Gas tank was part of frame; you pedaled to start.

The 1928 Cleveland, below, and 1929 model at right, are the rarest fours of all. Produced for only three years, company succumbed in crash of 1929.

The Harley-Davidson 74

This is the one that outlived every other American-made motorcycle to become (with its companion 55-cubic-inch model) the sole surviving example of the vee-twin breed. Its maker is, of course, the only remaining American manufacturer of motorcycles.

The Harley-Davidson 74 dates from the early 1920s when it was a product of the Milwaukee firm's quest for more power from their 61-cubic-inch twin, mainstay of their production during the very early years. More power was obtained in the simplest possible way—by enlarging the engine displacement to 74 cubic inches. The basic design remained unchanged: an F-head (inlet-over-exhaust) vee twin with the cylinders at a 45-degree angle on a vertically split crankcase. The gearbox is separate, has three speeds, and is hand-shifted. Clutch is a multiple-disc dry-plate type on the countershaft. Both primary and final drive are by single-row roller chain. Carburetor is a Schebler, ignition by Harley-Davidson coil and six-volt battery. The leading-link front fork has coil springing; the rear frame is rigid. Harley's patented

spring-loaded seat post provided much greater rider comfort than the Indian design. Controls are a right-hand twist-grip throttle, left foot rocker-pedal clutch, right foot rear brake, left-hand twist-grip control of the spark advance. The machine was big and somewhat clumsy in appearance; but it was reliable, tracked well, and gave good service.

From its inception until 1929, Harley continued this model basically without change. In 1925 a much more pleasing appearance was achieved with a well-streamlined saddle-type gas tank, and in 1929 a front-wheel brake was added. Other detail refinements had been made each year and the 1929 model was the culmination of many years of concentration on the F-head type of power plant. At this point, Harley-Davidson made a radical change in engine design.

The 1930 Harley-Davidson announcement described an entirely new 74 with a side-valve engine of simple, rugged design that was to render excellent service for many years. These machines were notable for their tremendous torque, and were mechanically quiet and smooth-running. In later years, an 80-cubic-inch version was offered. Personally I liked the 74 side-valver better than any other machine Milwaukee ever made, before or since.

In 1936 Harley introduced a new 61 cubic-inch overhead-valve model which later was enlarged to 74 inches—again in the quest for more power. This 1936-model 61 is the direct ancestor of today's 74 and the design has not been radically altered since. Through the ensuing years, 31 of them, Harley has made many improvements in the machine. And today it may very possibly be the most reliable motorcycle power plant in the world. In recent years the addition of a good spring frame and a self-starter have given this grand American a renewed lease on life.

American Fours

Four-cylinder motorcycles have always been of great interest to me, and to many other motorcyclists, because of their easy starting, smooth running and unobtrusive exhaust note, which usually made them more acceptable in "nice" neighborhoods. And, an added bonus, they were unexciting to our canine friends. This last was, and is, important—as any rider who has been successfully pursued by a dog will testify.

Aside from the Pierce Four (derived from the Belgian FN) and the 1926 Cleveland T-head (Fowler Four) designs, all of the commercially produced American fours have a common beginning.*

In 1912 the very first Henderson Four made its appearance; it was the work of William and Tom Henderson of Detroit. Their Henderson Motorcycle Co. continued production in Detroit until 1917.

The first Henderson was an odd-looking motorcycle, with an extremely long wheelbase, cylindrical tank, and aluminum foot plate. The engine was an F-head type; the transmission was single speed. In 1914 a shorter, more conventional frame was introduced along with a two-speed gearbox.

* Two other four-cylinder American motorcycles were made, but in extremely small quantities. The Militor and Champion were both large, clumsy, and had automobile-type wood-spoked wheels. The Militor had small assist wheels that were lowered to hold the machine up when it stopped.

The 1912 Henderson, above, was granddaddy of most American fours. Tiny in-line cylinders, left, had carburetor and exhaust manifolds as in auto.

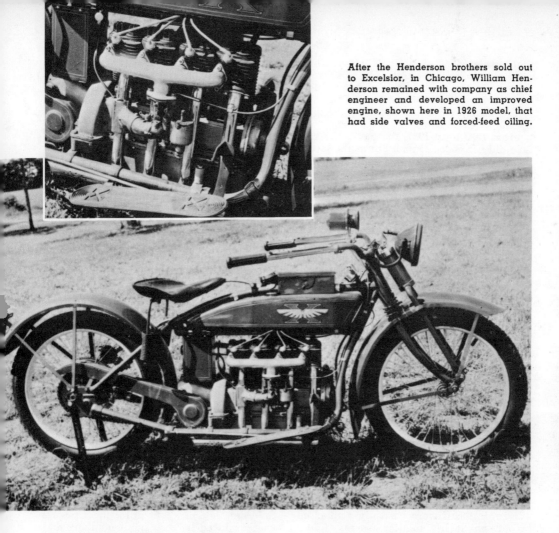

The 1917 model featured a three-speed gearbox with wet-sump oiling, and in the same year the Hendersons sold out to Excelsior in Chicago.

Manufacturing operations were moved there, with William Henderson as chief engineer on the fours. Excelsior lost no time in developing an improved engine with side valves and forced-feed oiling. This was continued until 1929, when another complete redesign was done by Arthur Constantine. The result was a beautifully streamlined KJ model—another F-head type which was continued until the Excelsior factory ceased production early in 1931. Even today, a well restored KJ Henderson is often mistaken for a modern motorcycle.

A flash-back to 1919 finds the Henderson brothers, Bill and Tom, leaving Excelsior and joining with Philadelphia interests to found a new company. With Henderson as chief engineer, the Ace Motor Co. brought out a fine new four-cylinder motorcycle, with many similarities to the earlier F-head Hendersons. The Ace, with its 77-cubic-inch engine, was a lighter motorcycle than the Henderson, and was capable of extremely good performance. Many Ace machines were manufactured and sold. But the company failed in 1924, and after some abortive efforts to get the machine back into production, the company's entire assets were bought by Indian in 1927. Indian produced the machine as the Indian Ace through 1928 with almost no change except adoption of Indian Red as the standard color.

In 1929, Indian revised the frame layout of the Ace and brought forth the first Indian Four. In 1930, a further redesign gave the machine a five-bearing crankshaft and much-improved reliability.

These 401 series Indian Fours employed the same graceful tank and frame lines as the 101 Scout, and were good-looking motorcycles. Not exceptionally fast, they were sold in limited numbers in a difficult, depression era. In 1932 a further redesign was undertaken—confined almost entirely to the frame, which was much larger than the 401 type.

From 1932 until 1937, the basic Ace engine did not change much but in the latter year, a serious mistake was made in modifying the engine to an exhaust-over-inlet type employing two up-draught carburetors. This proved to be an unreliable engine and the very next year saw the almost entirely new Indian Four, which was continued with detail changes until the end of its production in 1941.

Another flashback returns us to 1927 when the Cleveland Motorcycle Manufacturing Co. of that Ohio city embarked on production of a 61-cubic-inch four-cylinder machine that was strongly influenced by the work of Henderson. This was not surprising because the engineer, E. M. DeLong, had worked with Henderson in the Ace factory in Philadelphia. The new Cleveland 61-cubic-inch motorcycle followed earlier 45- and 37-cubic-inch efforts that proved inadequate. Cleveland Fours were produced in 1927, 1928, and for a short time in 1929—when the factory failed. Today they are quite rare, the hardest to find of any four-cylinder machine described here.

Summarizing, there were four Henderson-inspired four-cylinder motorcyes: the Henderson (79 cu. in.), Ace (77 cu. in.), Cleveland (61 cu. in.), and Indian Four (77 cu. in.). All were basically similar in layout, employing tubular frames, four-cylinders-in-line engines, wet-sump lub-

rication, engine-speed clutches, three-speed gearboxes, and bevel-gear-to-chain final drive. The last of the series, the 1941 Indian Four, reached quite monumental physical proportions, but was quite reliable and capable of a fair turn of speed. A relatively large number of these machines still exists.

Never produced was the intended 1946 Indian Four. This was a 61-cubic-inch ohv design with down-draught carburetor situated in the dummy left-side gas tank. In the prototype, owned by Clinton Feld of Brooklyn, shaft drive was employed with a foot shift and hand clutch.

Another "intended" that never made it into production was the 1948 Indian Torque Four. This was to have been a part of the modular series envisioned by the Rogers interests when they brought out the lightweight vertical twin and light single in 1949. This four-cylinder machine (the prototype of which still exists) was to have been a 48-cubic-inch model employing many of the same parts as the single and the twin. The prototype does, in fact, have four single-type cylinders and a shaft drive.

Cyclone

Then there was the Cyclone. Never before, and seldom after, has there been a motorcycle so surrounded by mystery, legend, and stories of its fabulous capabilities. And the Cyclone deserved much of that acclaim.

Born under obscure circumstances in St. Paul, Minn., about 1913, the Cyclone was produced in very small numbers and only for two or three years; it went out of

The Ace, shown here in the 1922 model, was yet another four developed by Henderson that became popular because of its excellent performance.

At left and above is the 1939 model of the Indian four whose engine had been developed in 1938; was produced with only detail changes until 1941.

production during the 1915 season. But in that brief span the Cyclone became the terror of the dirt tracks!

In the hands of Don Johns, a daring and fearless track rider of the era, a Cyclone dirt tracker literally ran away from the factory machines fielded by Indian, Harley-Davidson, and Excelsior. A combination of light weight and good riding were partly responsible, but Cyclone power, the result of very clever engine design, was the main reason.

The Cyclone engine (known as the Strand engine after designer Andrew Strand) is a 61-cubic-inch vee twin with a 42-degree angle between cylinders and a vertically split crankcase. Cylinders are steel castings, as are the heads. Valves are quite large, being 1¾ inches in diameter, set at a 70-degree angle in true hemispherical combustion chambers. Valves are actuated by single overhead camshafts through rockers. An ingenious yoke arrangement exerts a "pull down" effect on the valve stems, eliminating side-thrust. Compression ratio is 5.5 to 1. Peak rpm is 5,000 and the speeds attained on the track suggest an output of about 40 hp. The connecting rods run on three rows of caged roller bearings, the timing side has a two-row self-aligning ball bearing, and the drive side boasts no less than four rows of caged roller bearings. The entire crank and flywheel assembly is very narrow for increased rigidity.

The camshafts are driven by bevel-geared vertical shafts and the Bosch magneto is similarly driven. A mechanical oil pump provides lubrication by the total loss system.

The Cyclone factory insisted on extreme accuracy, and no shims were used to obtain the correct end-play in the crank and flywheel assembly. The entire engine was hand fitted and all castings were beautifully polished.

A relatively few road-model Cyclones appeared employing a front fork strikingly similar to the Indian leaf-spring type. A novel swinging-arm rear frame was controlled by a leaf-spring mounted vertically behind the seat post. Standard color, a violent yellow, earned it the nickname of "The Yellow Peril," especially from competitors on the dirt tracks.

Today the Cyclone is an extremely rare

bird. One of the existing models, owned by Robert Lyons of Chicago, has a most interesting history. Lyons was once interested in helping revive the Cyclone in the early 1920s. The project fell through but netted him one new road model, later stripped for use as a track racer. This machine lay in Lyons cellar for many years until, quite recently, he decided to rebuild it as a road model. Unfortunately, all the road parts—spring frame, fenders, handlebars, etc.—had long since disappeared.

Lyons faced the prospect of making parts for which he had no plans or even photographs. But in his search for information he returned to the Cyclone's birthplace, St. Paul, and stumbled onto the kind of "impossible" luck that makes truth stranger than fiction. In 1961, more than half-a-century after the Cyclone was born, he found a very old gentleman who had drafted the plans for Andy Strand's engine as a young man in 1910. Sewell was his name and, still hale and hearty, he drew up a new set of plans for the road parts—entirely from memory. Today, it is said, the gleamingly restored road Cyclone stands in a place of honor in Bob Lyon's Chicago office.

The Flying Merkel

It was always called *The* Flying Merkel. That's how the factory-applied decal on the original orange-enamelled tank of my own machine reads. The marque and the motorcycle have very interesting things to be said about them. Long years ago the last "Yellow Jacket" rolled out of the factory in Middletown, Ohio, but once upon a time the future looked bright for the Merkel. Its exact birthdate is somewhat hazy, but it's known that Joe Merkel was making machines in Milwaukee about 1905. About 1909 Merkel merged with the Light Motor Co. of Pottstown, Pa. and became chief engineer of the newly formed Merkel-Light Motor Co.

From 1909 to 1911 Merkel-Light manufactured a variety of single- and twin-cylinder models featuring automatic intake valves and an ingenious spring frame. In 1910 or early 1911 the Merkel-Light Motor Co. was bought by the Miami Cycle and Manufacturing Co. of Middletown, Ohio, and all operations moved with Joe Merkel to that city. Miami had been making bicycles, and their own Racycle motorcycle, for some years with indifferent suc-

The Cyclone was a fabulous motorcycle, almost entirely hand produced between 1913 and 1915. It ran away from competition on dirt tracks because of light weight and power, the result of clever engine design.

1914 CYCLONE
(specifications)

Engine type: Four-stroke, ohc vee-twin
Displacement: 1,000 cc (61 cu. in.)
Bore/stroke: $3\frac{5}{16}$ in. x $3\frac{1}{32}$ in.
Horsepower: 40 @ 5,000 rpm (est.)
Ignition: magneto
Top speed: road model 85 mph
track model 95-100 mph
Speeds: 1   Weight: 220 lbs. (est.)
Miles/gallon: 50 Tires: (Not available)

The Merkel was another fabulous machine which became known as The Flying Merkel. The 1914 model here had a 61-cubic-inch F-head engine with unusually large valves. Oiling was by hand pump.

1914 FLYING MERKEL
(specifications)
Engine type:
Four-stroke, F-head vee-twin
Displacement: 1,000 cc (61 cu. in.)
Bore/stroke: 3¼ in. x 3⁴⁵/₆₄ in.
Horsepower: 15   Ignition: Magneto
Top speed: 60 mph (est.)
Tires: 3.00x21 clincher
Speeds: 1 or 2   Miles/gallon: 50
Weight: 225 lbs. (est.)

---

cess. In Merkel they had a well-known name and at first made progress in building their business.

Standard color was a garish orange, though dark blue could be ordered specially. There was much nickel plating on *The* Flying Merkel, as it was then being called, and Miami continued to make them until 1915.

The Flying Merkel twin of 1914 has a 61-cubic-inch F-head engine. Valves were unusually large for the time. All cam and magneto drive gears run on ball bearings, as do the connecting rods. Main bearings are also ball-type. Oiling is by hand pump and adjustable drip feed. (Strangely, Merkel abandoned a mechanical pump used on older models.) Standard transmission is single speed, though a two-speed version was available. There are bicycle pedals if you run out of gas.

A tube-and-lug frame makes a full loop under the engine. The oil tank is built into the seat post. An ingenious spring frame—a true swinging arm—is pivoted on a large five-inch diameter bushing with a built-in grease gun. Springing is by a large spring

housed in a tube under the saddle—very similar to the scheme adopted years later by the British-made Vincent. The front fork is a truss type with limited springing at the steering head. This fork was much favored by dirt track riders of the day and was often fitted to Indian racers. The Merkel's rear wheel was quickly detachable without removing the chain, a rarity.

Like many other motorcycle manufacturers, Miami was forced out of business by the new Model T Ford. It continued to make bicycles, however, and in 1917 brought out the Miami Power Cycle. This throwback to a primitive motorcycle had a single cylinder, flat belt and jockey-pulley drive. It failed.

Literally hundreds of other makes of motorcycles were manufactured in the United States between 1901 and 1930. If you're interested, some libraries in the larger cities have bound volumes of old American motorcycle magazines: *The Motorcycle, Motorcyclist and Bicyclist,* and *Motorcycling.* They contain thousands of pages of text and pictures that describe an exciting, half-forgotten era. •

A Treasury of British Motorcycles

By Denis Wilson

PICKING A SMALL number of outstanding British-built motorcycles from the 550-odd recorded makes over the years is an invidious occupation—one likely to gain more enemies than friends.

Besides, any such Hall of Fame will, inevitably, be more notable for its omissions than content. For instance, the 1919 ABC, before-its-time in many respects, has a strong case for inclusion. It boasted such "modern" features as a transverse-twin OHV engine with hemispherical heads, plus a unit gearbox set in a sprung frame of duplex construction.

And is one really justified in ignoring the engineering marvels of the performance-plus 998 cc Vincent . . . .?

However, the final choice has been made because each machine listed represents a particular niche carved in the history of British motorcycles.

1933 Brough Superior 680

"The Rolls-Royce of Motorcycles" was one very satisfied owner's description of his Brough Superior in 1921, and the slogan was later taken up by a journalist writing about the Brough in a British motorcycling weekly. Shortly, George Brough

---

1933 BROUGH Superior 680
(specifications)
Engine type: V-twin OHV
Displacement: 674 cc (41 cu. in.)
Bore/stroke: 70 x 88 mm
Horsepower: 25 @ 4,500 rpm
Ignition: Magneto   Top speed: 84
Compression: 7 to 1
Speeds: 4   Miles/gallon: 45 to 50
Weight: Approx. 490 lbs.
Tires: Front—3.50x26   Rear—4.00x27

Called "The Rolls-Royce of Motorcycles" for its high standards of engineering, the Brough held 13 world flying-kilometer and miles records between 1924 and 1937. The "680" had Castle front forks.

Probably the most successful and best-loved racing motorcycle ever, Norton's Manx became synonomous with the Isle of Man Tourist Trophy. Norton singles started the ball rolling with cammy models.

1949 NORTON Manx 30M and 40M
(specifications)

Engine type:
Single cylinder—double overhead camshaft

Displacement:
348 cc (21 cu. in.) and 499 cc (30.5 cu. in.)

Bore/stroke: (30M)—76 x 76.7 mm
(40M)—86 x 95.6 mm

Horsepower: (30M)—41 @ 8,200 rpm
(40M)—51 @ 7,600 rpm

Tires: Front—3.00x19   Rear—3.50x19

Ignition: Magneto

Top speed: (30M)—112 mph
(40M)—116 mph

Compression: (30M) 11 to 1
(40M) 10.6 to 1

Speeds: 4   Miles/gallon: 35

Weight: (30M)—307 lbs.
(40M)—313 lbs.

---

was including the accolade in his advertizements, with the tacit approval of Rolls-Royce themselves.

The comparison had its points, for the renowned Broughs were built regardless of cost and to a very high standard (by any standards) of engineering. Nor were they found lacking in the performance departments, the big 1,000 cc V-twins were especially noted for speed. Between 1924 and 1937, Broughs held 13 World flying-kilometer and mile records.

The most favored Brough Superiors were the JAP-engined V-twins, ranging from 680 cc to 1,000 cc, including a 1,000 side-valve model—the last word in tractability. The "680" illustrated here was for Brough clients (you could not call Brough riders *customers*) without bottomless pockets. Though the small model lacked only the cc's of its bigger brothers it enjoyed the same superb roadholding which was aided and abetted by the unusual Castle front forks.

In 1949 BSA Gold Stars were fitted for telescopic front forks and plunger-type rear springing. This later was altered to the current vogue of swinging fork. Now, BSAs are obtainable only on special order.

1949 BSA Gold Star (specifications)		
Engine type: Single cylinder OHV	Ignition: Magneto	Weight: 365 lbs.
Displacement: 348 cc (21 cu. in.) and 499 cc (30.5 cu. in.)	Top speed: (348)—105 mph (499)—110 mph	
Bore/stroke: (348)—71 x 88 mm (499)—85 x 88 mm	Compression: (348) 8.75 to 1 (499) 8 to 1	
Horsepower: (348)—32 @ 7,500 rpm (499)—38 @ 7,000 rpm	Speeds: 4 Miles/gallon: 40 to 50 Tires: Front—3.00x19 Rear—3.50x19	

Like many high-powered, high-performance, high-priced motorcycles, the Brough Superior went down to the post-World War II society's lust for automobiles and its production was not resumed after the war. But it will always be remembered as one of the great (if not the *greatest*) products of the British motorcycle industry.

1949 Norton Manx 30M and 40M

In 1928, the Birmingham-based Norton company introduced its CS1 overhead-camshaft racing engine, from which the world-famous Manx racers were evolved. The Manxes were to become the most successful road racing models of all time, and synonymous with the Isle of Man Tourist Trophy—the world's greatest road race. In fact, founder J. L. Norton had seen his marque score a first in the twin-cylinder class of the first-ever Tourist Trophy in 1907, but that model was fitted with a French Peugeot engine. The famous Norton singles added another 33 "island" victories, really starting the ball rolling in 1931 with the "cammy" models.

Time after time, as Nortons staved off challenges from more exotic invaders, the basic soundness of design was proved with more TT wins. The last came in 1961, when Mike Hailwood won the 500 cc race on a Manx. Then, finally, came the eclipse from the highly specialized products of Italy and Japan.

In 1950, the racing Nortons arrived equipped with "featherbed" frames, giving them a standard of control like no motorcycle had known before—and, some insist,

The Scott has often been called "The Father of Modern Two-Stroke Twins." Though production ceased at the Yorkshire plant in 1950, Scotts are still available on request from Birmingham tool makers.

since. From the early post-World War II years, until their production ceased in 1963, the Manxes were sold as catalogued "production racers." To this day, on circuits throughout the world, private owners are still chalking up "Manx" successes. Truly, the most successful, most loved racing motorcycle ever.

1949 BSA Gold Star

Of all the well-known, well-liked British OHV "singles" which poured forth from the early thirties onwards, the Gold Stars were undoubtedly the most versatile. First introduced in 1937, the "Goldie" became available in trials, scrambles and racing form. Also, after the war, a special version was supplied for U.S. flat-tracking, proving very popular and successful. During the same period at home, Gold Stars made a terrific impact on British Clubman road-racing (racing with standard production machines). So dominant were the "Beesas" that the Clubman formula was scrapped, as it had become a "one-make benefit."

For 1949, Gold Stars were fitted with telescopic front forks and plunger-type rear springing, which later was altered to the current vogue of swinging fork. In 1958, the models became obtainable only on special order and the writing was clearly on the wall for production to be chopped in 1964—BSA's losing many friends in the process.

> ## 1957 SCOTT Flying Squirrel
> (specifications)
> **Engine type: Two stroke, parallel-twin**
> **Bore/stroke: 73 x 71 mm**
> **Horsepower: 30 @ 5,000 rpm**
> **Ignition: Coil and battery**
> **Top speed: 80 mph**
> **Compression: 6 to 1 (est.)**
> **Speeds: 3   Miles/gallon: 50**
> **Weight: 390 lbs.**
> **Tires: Front—3.25x19   Rear—3.50x19**

Back in 1937, the prototype lapped the famous Brooklands race course at 107.5 mph, for which feat it was awarded the prized Brooklands Gold Star. Hence the name.

Besides having many followers in its specialized sporting guises, the Gold Star was much sought-after as a potent sporting street bike, at a time when "big singles" were very much "in." Its supporters were apt to consider the vertical twin somewhat effeminate. Certainly, the Gold Star was a man's model with many commendable features.

1957 Scott Flying Squirrel

Alfred Angus Scott was, despite his name, bred in Yorkshire and developed an unconventional engineering brain which he used to design motorcycles. That, so

First introduced in 1930 as an overhead (chain-driven) camshaft five-hundred, the Ariel grew to 600 cc and finally emerged as a push-rod overhead-valve thousand. Later it had all-aluminum engines.

Yorkshiremen will tell you, is reason enough for including Alfred's products in this review. A more objective view would put it that Scott endowed the two-stroke engine with some much-needed sophistication. Although the very early Scott engines were air-cooled, when production started in 1909 his twin-cylinder two-strokes appeared in the water-cooled form that gained them world-wide fame—and that has been the way of things ever since. At the same time, an open-loop frame was developed, proving to be miles ahead of the bicycle-type contraptions then popular—if that is the right word.

Scotts are delightful bikes to ride, having more in common with the modern Japanese two-stroke multis than with the utilitarian "poppers" of the 1920's and 30's. The engines have always been noted for their ease of maintenance—pulling them apart is almost ridiculously simple.

A. A. Scott left the firm in 1919, but did the right thing by selling out to a group of fellow Yorkshiremen. They naturally stuck with the two-stroke twin configuration; the engine remaining basically unaltered apart from continued updating and changes in capacities until 1936, when it was finalized. Even now, Scotts are still available by special request from a Birmingham firm of tool makers, though production ceased at the Yorkshire plant in 1950.

The Scott has often been called "The Father of Modern Two-Stroke Twins"—a worthy description that cannot be bettered.

1958 ARIEL 4G Square Four
(specifications)

Engine type: Four cylinder, OHV
Displacement: 997 cc (61 cu. in.)
Bore/stroke: 65 x 75 mm
Horsepower: 50 @ 6,000 rpm
Ignition: Coil and battery
Top speed: 97 mph   Weight: 435 lbs.
Compression: 7.2 to 1
Speeds: 4   Miles/gallon: 40
Tires: Front—3.25x19   Rear—4.00x18

1958 Ariel 4G Square Four

The trouble with most four-cylinder machines is their expensive complexities. Thus, most prewar "fours," especially those owing much to car-type engineering practices, were short-lived affairs. But the Ariel "Square-Four," designed by Edward Turner (later responsible for the Triumph Twin), overcame the handicap simply by being a square-four! This layout was compact enough to allow a normal offset primary drive, conventional clutch and separate gearbox. So the Ariel was able to enjoy a life-span of nearly 30 years before going the way of all British "thousands" in 1959.

The "Squariel's" great pride and joy was its wonderfully docile power impulses resulting from a modest 7.2 to 1 compression ratio. In addition, the mechanical balance was of very high order; two 180-degree

Panthers and sidecars go together like ham and eggs and are distinguished by their big sloping engines, instead of normal down tube. Its 1958 version was the biggest-capacity single, at 645 cc.

```
1959 PANTHER 100 and 120S
(specifications)
Engine type: Single-cylinder OHV
Displacement: (100) — 598 cc (36 cu. in.)
             (120S) — 645 cc (39 cu. in.)
Bore/stroke: (100) — 87 x 100 mm
             (120S) — 87 x 106 mm
Horsepower: 25 @ 4,500 rpm
Ignition: Magneto      Top speed: 70 mph
Speeds: 4     Miles/gallon: 50 to 60
Compression: 6.5 to 1     Weight: 426 lbs.
Tires: Front — 3.50x19     Rear — 3.50x19
```

vertical twins, in effect geared together, produced the desired result.

First introduced in 1930 as an overhead (chain-driven) camshaft five-hundred, the Ariel grew to 600 cc and finally emerged as a push-rod overhead-valve thousand. The later versions had all-aluminum engines, neatly fitted into frames which featured telescopic forks and an unusual short-link rear suspension arrangement.

With a top speed near the magic "ton" (100 mph) and a safe bottom speed (in top gear) of 13 mph, the Ariel's performance range would fit every need. Unfortunately, in its latter years it could not fit the contemporary pay envelopes!

1959 Panther 100 and 120S

It often surprises the younger motorcycling generations to learn there was once a thriving British sidecar industry. More-over, there were motorcycle manufacturers content to make bikes exclusively for the sidecar clan. Indeed, some people favored sidecar outfits, not merely as a low-cost substitute for cars, but as alternatives. They were encouraged with a lower road tax rate, and by insurance companies who rated the two-track oddities as the safest things on wheels.

Sidecar luggers, by popular demand, were deemed to require the characteristics of steam engines: to be able to tow whole families and piles of luggage around with minimal fuss, to chug up any hill, to burble happily along the flat without ever getting out of top gear. So, big-capacity side-valve twins and singles were often given the job. They were rivalled by the large OHV single with a big, beefy piston which trotted up and down in yards of cylinder. Like the Panther.

Panthers and sidecars went (and go) together like ham and eggs, and are easily distinguishable by their big sloping engines. It all came about because Harry Rayner, Jonah Phaelon and Richard Moore were so horrified at the inadequacies of the 1900 "motorcycle" frame that they stuck a sloping engine in place of the normal down tube. It stuck to such purpose that when the Panther OHV single "sloper" was introduced, it went on to collect the honor of being one of the machines longest in continuous production in the world. Also, it was the biggest-capacity single, at 645 cc, in a version introduced for 1958.

As fashions changed, the demand for

Panthers dwindled to a point where quantity production was no longer worth while. Now, Panthers are only available on special order.

A ride on a Panther is a reminder of more specious days, and a never-to-be-forgotten experience if you try it in solo form.

1937 Triumph Speed Twin

When Edward Turner designed his 1937 parallel-twin Triumph, he not only started a craze, but laid the foundations for what was to become *the* British motorcycle. Soon after the wartime shutdown, every major British make (BSA, Ariel, Norton, A.J.S., Matchless, Royal Enfield) listed vertical twins. But none of them were actually able to dislodge Triumphs from the top of the popularity poll.

The 1937 Triumph was (engine apart) typical of British two-wheeler engineering of that period with its low saddle, girder forks, mag-dyno electrics, separate engine and gearbox, and general air of sportiness.

Postwar work saw the introduction of an unsuccessful rear sprung hub and partial enclosure of the rear, which was only notable for creating a huge consumer resistance. These slips apart, the Triumph gained a reputation for being internationally popular. In 1949, a 649 cc version was introduced, largely at the insistence of American Triumph dealers. Improved-performance twins followed at regular annual intervals, but in 1958 it was thought

wise to modernize the 500 cc Speed Twin engine by making it over-square (69 x 65 mm) and in unit with the gearbox. Handling remained somewhat "iffish" until comparatively recently when major frame and fork alterations effected a complete cure.

Judged the best of its type anywhere, and the most popular British motorcycle overseas, the Triumph has that indefinable something which gives it a head start over its rivals. Undoubtedly a "must" in my list.

There, then, are seven famous British motorcycles—and a potted history of motorcycling in the United Kingdom. The models of the early "pedal assistance" era have been deliberately left out, for many motorcycles then were what we may call gimmick expressions of enthusiastic hopes and ideals—often coming down with a sickening thud in practice. Only those

---

**1937 TRIUMPH Speed Twin
(specifications)**
Engine type: Parallel vertical twin, OHV
Displacement: 497 cc (30.5 cu. in.)
Bore/stroke: 63 x 80 mm
Horsepower: 26 @ 6,000 rpm
Ignition: Magneto   Top speed: 94 mph
Compression: 7.2 to 1   Speeds: 4
Miles/gallon: 55   Weight: 365 lbs.
Tires: Front—3.00x20   Rear—3.50x19

Vertical twins became the order of the day when Turner designed his 1937 Triumph. It also featured low saddle, girder forks, mag-dyno electrics, separate engine and gearbox, and a look of sportiness.

motorcycles, like Brough and Scott, based on the soundest engineering principles were able to survive into the mid-twenties and onward.

It is a sobering thought that of all the bikes described, only the Triumph is still properly with us. And, significantly, there is no British lightweight worthy of consideration. Perhaps it would have been a different story if the 250 cc Ariel Leader of 1958 had been introduced earlier. The Leader combined scooter-type all-weather protection, with the scale and roadholding of a full-size motorcycle employing a two-stroke twin engine. It was envisaged as putting large sections of populations safely on two wheels in the crowded commuter age. Alas, the scooter boom crashed, and motorcyclists poo-hooed the idea of enclosure. Those who sought weather protection took advantage of the European mini-car explosion. Those in sunnier environments insisted their chromeplated and polished engines should shine forth, uninhibited by covers.

As for the pictures illustrating this article, the motorcycles are not always shown in their original or early forms. The Triumph Twin is, but the 1933 Brough Superior is shown to display the elegance of that period. As for the Panther and Scott pictures, the choice is dictated by the de-

The Leader combined scooter-type all-weather protection, with the scale and roadholding of a full-size cycle employing 2-stroke twin engine.

ARIEL Leader
(specifications)
Engine type: Parallel-twin, two stroke
Displacement: 247 cc (15 cu. in.)
Bore/stroke 54 x 54 mm
Horsepower: 17 @ 6,400 rpm
Ignition: Coil and battery
Top speed: 70 mph   Weight: 330 lbs.
Compression: 8.25 to 1
Speeds: 4   Miles/gallon: 45
Tires: Front—3.25x16   Rear—3.25x16

---

sire to show how old engines can be presented in new packages (i.e. spring frames) to advantage. The Gold Star depicts the transition from prewar design to postwar embellishments. Its engine has yet to grow the large cylinder finning of later years, while the basically 1939 frame is adapted to take telescopic forks and plunger-type rear springing. Finally, the Norton Manx picture proves how tough road racing must have been, prefeatherbed. •

Inside Motorcycle Engines

SELDOM BEFORE in motorcycle history has so much attention been lavished on engine design. Today motorcyclists have an unprecedented range of types to choose from. Illustrated and described here are the nine basic ones now available.

The engines fall into three broad groups: time-honored road mills gradually honed to a fine edge; once-exotic racing powerplants translated into mass-produced form; and pussycat performers transformed into tigers by major improvements.

Each type of engine has its own special constellation of characteristics that balance performance, efficiency, and reliability in varying amounts. Fortunately the versatility of motorcycle engines matches the versatility of the sport itself, with certain engines especially adaptable to certain kinds of riding.

But even if all motorcycles were used for only one purpose—like traveling by road from A to B—the variety would greatly appeal to any motorcyclist. More aware of his engine than an automobile driver, he's aware of its unique personality: the two-stroke twin's turbine-like pull under load, the OHC four-stroke's swift rise to the top of the rpm scale, the big V-twin's raw power surge. Each type requires its own special handling if it's to give maximum performance and reliability. Knowing how an engine works is a good first step toward acquiring that skill.

Veteran riders will applaud one recent piece of good news. The venerable side-valve V-twin, its production suspended over a decade ago, will again be available. Motorcycle pioneer Floyd Clymer, in collaboration with a German factory, is building a 45 cu. in. Indian Scout.

Clymer also offers a four-cylinder machine; but it's unlikely to be mass-produced at $4,000 a copy. Americans still feel an intense nostalgia for this breed and the first manufacturer to offer one at a reasonably popular price will undoubtedly sell all he can make. *Are you listening, Mr. Soichiro Honda?*

Following are the nine types of engines available.

Piston-Port, Two-Stroke Single

Once the pussycat of motorcycle engines, the piston-port, two stroke has been transformed into a tiger by making detail improvements in the single-cylinder layout and by joining two cylinders side by side to form a twin.

The sequence of events in all piston-port cylinders is the same. As the piston rises toward top dead center it creates a vacuum in the crankcase below and its skirt uncovers the intake port. Air rushes through

PISTON PORT, TWO-STROKE SINGLE
Typically a small-displacement engine, it was
used in the 175 cc Harley Davidson Scat machine.

the carburetor—picking up gasoline vapor
on the way—and passes through the intake
port into the crankcase. Meanwhile, the
piston compresses the previous charge
above it, the spark plug fires the mixture,
and the piston is driven downward.

On its downward trip the piston crown
first uncovers the exhaust port, out of
which burnt gases shoot into the exhaust
pipe. Slightly later, the crown uncovers
two transfer ports as well, and the new
charge, compressed by the bottom of the
downward-moving piston, swirls up out of

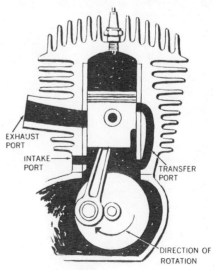

EXHAUST PORT

INTAKE PORT

TRANSFER PORT

DIRECTION OF ROTATION

the crankcase through the transfer passages and into the combustion chamber. Reversing direction at bottom dead center, the piston again slides upward, closing transfer and exhaust ports and opening the intake port to start another combustion cycle.

A slight variation occurs in the Bultaco, a Spanish-made motorcycle. It has a gas deflector plate which bounces incoming charges up transfer passages and into the combustion chamber fast, instead of letting the charge drift down into the crankcase. Dykes-type (L-shaped) piston rings, pressed against the cylinder wall by gas in the combustion chamber, permit high compression ratio and prevent blow-by past the piston on its work stroke.

Piston-Port, Two-Stroke Twin

The twin two-stroke has a separate carburetor and exhaust pipe for each cylinder. Pistons are connected 180° apart to a single crankshaft so that the cylinders fire alternately for greater smoothness. Most of these engines now have separate oiling systems, using pumps to feed the correct amount of oil to combine with the gasoline. Yamaha and Suzuki are leading makers of twin two-strokes.

Split-Single, Two-Stroke

A single combustion chamber has two bores, pistons, and connecting rods in the

engine. Offset on the same crankpin, con rods cause the pistons to move so that they are even at top and bottom dead center, and out of step in between. This permits an asymmetrical port timing that's impossible with the classic piston-port design.

As the pistons start upward on the compression stroke, the forward piston begins to lead slightly, uncovering the intake port when its skirt is about halfway up the barrel. A fresh charge rushes into the crankcase from the carburetor while the previous charge is being compressed in the barrel. At top dead center, with both pistons again even, the spark plug fires and the pistons are driven downward on the power stroke. The forward piston again takes the lead, more markedly this time, and about halfway down the barrel its crown uncovers the exhaust port.

Burnt gases begin rushing out into the tuned exhaust system, mostly from the forward half of the barrel. Not until the forward piston has completely uncovered the exhaust port does the rear piston begin to uncover the transfer port—now the two pistons are out of step the maximum amount. As the rear piston completely uncovers the transfer port both pistons—even once more—pause briefly at bottom dead center. The fresh charge spurts into the rear half of the cylinder, upward over the cylinder divider, and down into the forward half of the cylinder toward the ex-

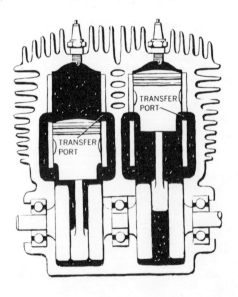

PISTON PORT, TWO-STROKE TWIN
Pairing two singles creates a potent powerplant for mediumweight bikes, like this 250 cc Yamaha.

haust port. As it follows this tortuous path, the fresh charge drives the remaining burnt gases out the exhaust port ahead of it.

Starting upward, the forward piston again takes the lead and closes the exhaust port before the rear piston closes the transfer port. Thus, fresh charge continues to flow into the combustion chamber after the exhaust port is covered, lengthening the filling period and preventing loss of fresh charge out the exhaust port, with tuned exhaust system's help.

Puch-Allstate makes the only engine of this design sold in the U.S.

Rotary-Valve, Two-Stroke Single

In this two-stroke, a vertical metal disc rotating at the end of the crankshaft, instead of an intake port, controls the movement of gasoline vapor from the carburetor to the crankcase.

A segment of the valve disc is cut away so that a fresh charge begins flowing into the crankcase as the piston starts upward on its compression stroke, then stops flowing soon after top dead center. The asymmetrical intake timing allows more charge in, while the exhaust port is closed, and less charge in, after that port opens, than a piston-controlled inlet port which must stay open an equal interval before and after top dead center.

Transfer and exhaust ports are piston-controlled as in a classical two-stroke. Absence of an intake port in the barrel of this engine makes possible a third transfer port that further speeds each fresh charge from crankcase to cylinder. In a twin-cylinder engine, pistons are 180° out of phase as in the piston-port twin.

A rotary valve is most common on single-cylinder two-strokes, with the valve on one end of the crankshaft and a magneto or generator on the other. On a twin, both crankshaft ends are masked by rotary valves; therefore alternator and ignition breaker-point cam are on a shaft behind the cylinders. This shaft is rotated at half engine speed by the timing gear, in mesh through an intermediate gear with a pinion gear on the crankshaft.

Yamaha, Bridgestone, and Kawasaki are leading makers of rotary-valve engines.

OHC Vertical Single

A timing shaft with spiral bevel gears on each end drives a single overhead camshaft in this engine. The bottom gear meshes with a pinion on the right end of the crankshaft and the top gear meshes with a bevel gear on the camshaft.

Inlet and exhaust cams on the camshaft nudge two rocker arms in sequence. Each arm pivots against a valve stem, opening the valve. As the cam lobe rotates out of contact with the rocker arm, pressure from a hairpin-type valve spring pushes the

SPLIT-SINGLE, TWO-STROKE
Two pistons moving out of phase in a single barrel is a unique feature of the 250 cc Puch-Allstate.

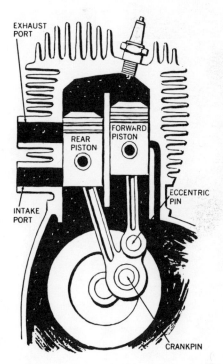

27

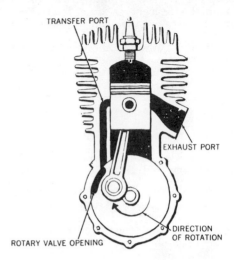

TRANSFER PORT

EXHAUST PORT

DIRECTION OF ROTATION

ROTARY VALVE OPENING

ROTARY-VALVE, TWO-STROKE SINGLE
Another, highly efficient, variation of the two-cycle engine powers the 175 cc Bridgestone bike.

valve stem down and closes the valve.

Ignition comes from a set of breaker points opened and closed by a cam on a spindle geared to the same crankshaft pinion that turns the timing shaft. A flywheel alternator turned by the left end of the crankshaft generates juice. The single domed piston rides up and down on the end of a connecting rod made fast to a pin between two central flywheels.

Ducati is the principal maker of this type of engine.

OHV Vertical Twin

Two upright cylinders are joined side by side. Though pistons go up and down together, plugs fire alternately to give one power pulse per engine revolution.

A timing gear—driven by a pinion gear on the crankshaft—controls valve and ignition timing for both cylinders. It simultaneously rotates an inlet camshaft aft of the crankshaft and an exhaust camshaft forward of it. A cam on one end of the exhaust camshaft opens and closes dual breaker points.

The camshafts operate four valves in sequence, two atop each cylinder, through push rods and rocker arms. As a cam lobe nudges the tappet of a push rod upward, the rod's upper end pivots a rocker arm against a valve stem. Stem and valve move downward, compressing a valve spring and uncovering the valve's seat. A fresh charge rushes into the cylinder if it's an inlet valve and burnt gases rush out if it's an exhaust valve. As the cam lobe rotates out from under the tappet, the push rod is pressed down again by valve-spring pressure acting through the rocker arm.

The intake and exhaust valves on each cylinder open and close once during a complete cycle of four strokes. The inlet valve opens on a downward piston stroke, allowing a fresh charge to be drawn in; both valves are closed on the upward compression stroke and remain so during the subsequent downward power stroke. The exhaust valve then opens on the upward exhaust stroke. This complete cycle takes two crankshaft revolutions.

Triumph, BSA, Norton and Kawasaki are leading manufacturers of vertical twins.

OHV singles work like one cylinder of a twin; some stand upright, others lie down fore and aft. They're made by BSA, Harley-Davidson, and Benelli.

OHV Flat Twin

In this engine, the pistons move in and out simultaneously in horizontally opposed cylinders; the cylinders are fired alternately.

A two-throw crankshaft—mounted fore and aft—drives an oil pump, generator, and camshaft through gears. The camshaft, in line above the crankshaft, operates four overhead valves through push rods and rocker arms in the usual four-stroke sequence. A magneto on the camshaft's front end supplies ignition voltage to a high-tension coil through cam-operated breaker points. Each cylinder has its own carburetor, supplied with air from a common air cleaner.

BMW has long been the only large manufacturer of this engine type. The Japanese made Marusho is a recent addition.

OHV V-Twin

This four-stroke has a 45° angle between cylinders to reduce the height of the large-displacement engine. Pistons go up and

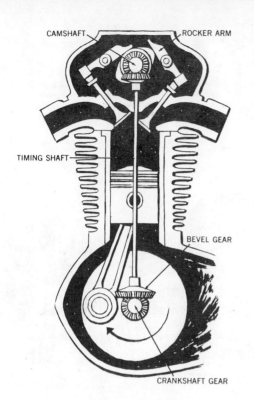

CAMSHAFT   ROCKER ARM

TIMING SHAFT

BEVEL GEAR

CRANKSHAFT GEAR

OHC VERTICAL SINGLE
Once common in racing machines, the overhead
camshaft single is used in the 250 cc Ducati Monza.

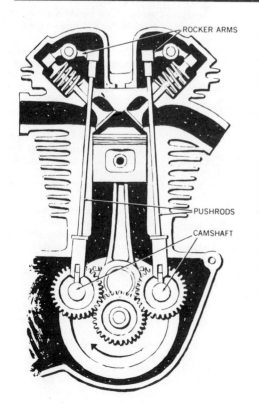

ROCKER ARMS

PUSHRODS

CAMSHAFT

OHV VERTICAL TWIN
Highly developed pushrod engine with two side-
by-side cylinders was pioneered by the Triumph.

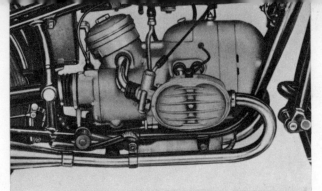

OHV FLAT TWIN
The horizontally opposed twin-cylinder powerplant has long been a monopoly of the BMW motorcycles.

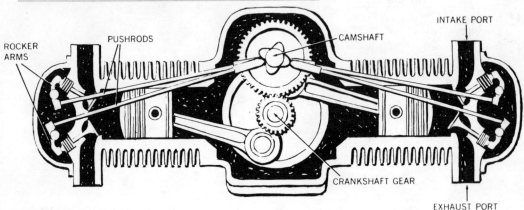

ROCKER ARMS · PUSHRODS · CAMSHAFT · INTAKE PORT · CRANKSHAFT GEAR · EXHAUST PORT

down together, their connecting rods joined at a common big-end whose bearing rides on a single crankpin between a pair of flywheels. Breaker points in an automobile-type distributor fire the cylinders alternately.

A single camshaft operates the four overhead valves in typical four-stroke sequence through push rods and rocker arms, while coiled valve springs maintain tension. To keep close contact between roller tappets and cams as its tall cylinders expand and contract with varying temperature, this engine has hydraulic lifters between tappets and push rods. The lifters —tiny spring- and oil-filled pistons with ball-check valves—change length as the distance between cams and rocker arms varies.

Harley-Davidson has long been the leading maker of V-twins.

DOHC Vertical-Twin

The pistons of this engine are 180° out of phase—one goes up while the other comes down—and each connecting rod rides between a pair of flywheels, drives a long timing chain that loops upward through a tunnel between the two cylinders, over sprockets on two overhead camshafts, and down again.

The exhaust and intake camshafts operate two valves atop each cylinder in typical four-stroke sequence. As a cam lobe moves into valve-opening position, it nudges a cam follower that presses down the valve-stem's stop. When the lobe moves out from under the cam follower, the valve stem is lifted up by a forked outer arm which is attached to a torsion-bar valve spring.

The pencil-sized torsion bar has splines on both ends: one end fits into a fixed locating bracket, the rest slides into a hollow tube that's splined inside. The tube has the outer arm fastened to its middle and is free to move. Pressing down on the valve stem twists the tube, creating tension inside the tube between the tube and torsion-bar splines. That tension later shoves the valve stem upward again, closing the valve.

Ignition timing is supplied by dual breaker points, a set for each cylinder, opened and close by a cam on the left-hand end of the exhaust camshaft. An alternator generates alternating current that's rectified to direct current and fed through high-tension coils to the spark plugs by the breaker points.

Honda is the only maker of this engine for general use. •

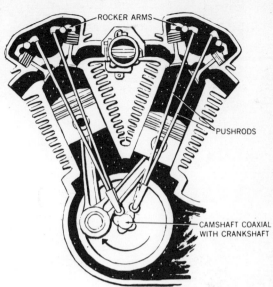

ROCKER ARMS

PUSHRODS

CAMSHAFT COAXIAL
WITH CRANKSHAFT

OHV V-TWIN
Spreading the cylinders apart in a V lowers engine height for the big 1,200 cc Harley-Davidson.

DOHC FOUR-STROKE TWIN
Once confined to expensive racing engines, double overhead camshaft distinguishes 450 cc Hondas.

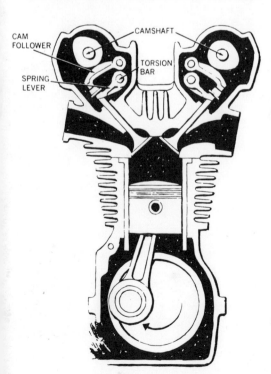

CAM FOLLOWER

CAMSHAFT

TORSION BAR

SPRING LEVER

Author and son with the seven-mount stable: trail bike, lightweight road bike, scrambler, sidecar outfit, enduro-trails machine, mediumweight and heavyweight touring bikes. They filled one side of the garage.

A Dream Stable of Motorcycles

INVENTING the pleasant fiction that money was no object, I assembled the mounts you see here. Without the generous help of dealers and importers it would have cost $7,626 (f.o.b.) to turn my dream into reality.

Choosing the stable turned out to be interesting, informative, and very personal. I found myself considering just about everything learned in 20 years of reading about, testing, and owning motorcycles.

Naturally, no two enthusiasts could expect to come up with the same list as mine. So if you're outraged, or just intrigued with the idea, write your own list. It's fun.

Honda Trail 90

My first meeting with this little wonder was several years ago when I tested seven trail bikes for a national magazine. It wasn't the largest, most powerful, or even most comfortable of the bunch. But it *was* an honest-to-goodness trail bike. It had an upswept pipe and spark-arresting muffler, skid plate, 5½-inch ground clearance, knobby tires, paper air cleaner mounted high up, steel front fender with clearance at top and mud flap at bottom, dual sprockets, and a large carrier.

All of these useful goodies were mounted on a sturdy step-through frame, so I could paddle through tough spots with both feet on the ground. And they were propelled by a tireless, quiet four-stroke engine working through an automatic clutch.

They've continued to improve the Trail 90 and this latest model is even better. The outstanding improvement is a device called "Posi-Torque," which allows you to switch from trail to street gearing and back in seconds. On my machine you simply flip a lever on the left side of the crankcase. This changes engine sprockets, eliminating the previous half-hour job of fooling with the rear chain and two rear-wheel sprockets. (A handlebar control is on the way.)

Now the trail bike is really a dual-purpose machine. I drove down to the store in street gear, then turned my older son loose in an overgrown vacant lot with the trail gear hooked in. On vacation the new feature would really pay off.

What makes the Honda Trail 90 so impressive is its unusual blend of genteel road-type conveniences with practical off-road features. Yet it was obviously designed from the knobby tires up as a trail machine, not converted like many others from road to trail use.

Take the battery. It makes the bike much easier to start; the horn really works, and the head and tail lights will burn brightly even when the engine's not running. Then there's a key-operated ignition switch and a fork lock. The large, easily read speedometer dial registers tenths of a mile and has a green neutral-indicator light and a red high-beam indicator light. You can put the center stand down from either side. I could go on.

Looking at the trail side, they've taken advantage of the missing clutch lever (automatic clutch, remember) to provide a rear-brake lever. Thus, you have hand-operated levers for both brakes so you needn't lose the use of the rear one just because you're paddling astride or running

HONDA TRAIL 90
Engine type: Four stroke, single cylinder, OHC
Displacement: 89.6 cc
Bore and stroke: 1.97 x 1.80 in. (50 x 45.6 mm)
Horsepower @ rpm: 7.0 @ 8,500 rpm
Compression Ratio: 8.2 : 1
Ignition: Battery
Top Speeds: 30/55 mph
Number of Speeds: Four
Miles per gallon: 165   Weight: 180 lbs.
Tires: Front—2.50x17   Rear—2.75x17
Price: $399 delivered Mineola, N.Y.

HONDA TRAIL 90

alongside with both feet busy. It's a great idea. The footrests fold if banged by a rock or log. Exhaust pipe and muffler are shielded by a perforated baffle so you won't get burned accidentally. There are even passenger footrests for any durable soul who would rather ride on a carrier than walk.

These features would be a waste, of

HONDA CB 160

Engine Type: Four stroke, twin cylinder, OHC
Displacement: 161 cc
Bore and stroke: 1.97 x 1.61 in.
(50 x 41 mm)
Horsepower @ rpm: 16.5 @ 10,000 rpm
Compression Ratio: 8.5 : 1   Ignition: Battery
Top Speed: 75 mph   Number of Speeds: Four
Miles per gallon: 116   Weight: 282 lbs.
Tires: Front — 2.50x18   Rear — 2.75x18
Price: $639 delivered Mineola, N.Y.

HONDA CB 160'

course, if the bike didn't go, handle, and stop well. It does all three. The single-cylinder overhead-camshaft engine pumps out seven horsepower without missing beats or screaming about it. The idle is even and it's virtually impossible, even for a beginner, to stall the engine. As soon as the load slows the engine down too much, the centrifugal clutch disengages. You just clamp on the very effective binders to stop and shift back to first at your leisure. Three of my youngsters have learned to ride without a mishap on the Trail 90. (The fourth is only seven.)

The four speeds are well spaced—first is a real stump puller in trail gearing. Top speed with the trail sprocket hooked in is 30 mph, a speed you seldom reach in really rough country. With the road gearing in operation you can go over 50. It doesn't hurt that you get up to 175 miles on each gallon of gas. A tank capacity of 1.7 gallons gives the bike a good range.

At first the centrifugal clutch seems like a mixed blessing, especially if you're used to a conventional one. You tackle a steep hill, for example, and half way up the going gets rough. Unexpectedly you're sitting there with a happy-sounding engine and a rear wheel that's doing nothing—the clutch decided to pull out. Normally you would have stalled the engine or slipped the clutch. But soon you get to like the easier shifting and find that by adjusting the clutch regularly you can go just about anywhere you want.

The brakes are typically Honda and can easily overpower clutch and engine, locking the wheels if you want them to. And you *may* want to lock the rear wheel if you're sliding down a steep hill. Locking just the front wheel at 20 mph, incidentally, brings the bike sliding to a stop in a straight line—a tribute to suspension and weight distribution. Speaking of weight, the machine's 180 pounds are a cinch to handle if you carry it on a trailer, in a bumper carrier, or inside a station wagon.

I'd like the Little Wonder even more if they'd jack up the ground clearance a bit and replace the suction cups under the seat with a latch so the seat doesn't fly up when you pull against the back of it. Other than that, Mr. Honda, revamp your lineup as much as you please but don't stop making that Trail 90.

Honda CB 160

I was frankly in awe of this little fellow's credentials when I rode it several years ago. After all it wasn't so long ago that any bike under 200 cc had to be a two-stroke. And few four-strokes under 500 cc had twin cylinders. Yet here was a twin-cylinder four-stroke, with an overhead camshaft no less, displacing a mere 160 cc.

It neatly filled a stall in my stable—the one reserved for a lightweight that's easy to handle, yet has enough juice to be exhilarating on twisty back roads without getting you into trouble. This is the bike for an hour's frisk near home when you're feeling relaxed and noncompetitive.

There's a trim, racy look to the Super Sport that apeals to me—the forward-sloping engine, twin carburetors, double-leading-shoe front brake, slim tight-fitting front fender, telescopic forks, and dual exhausts. Adding 12-volt battery ignition and an electric starter is almost too much. How sophisticated can a 160 get?

The machine lived up to its advance billing. If the battery is fully charged and both carburetors are in tune, a few seconds of pushing the starter button on the handlebar fires up the engine. It's a restrained, but potent sound, as it comes out of those effective mufflers. People hardly notice you, which is nice, too, sometimes.

Gently nudging the shift lever down into first, you let in a pleasingly light and smooth-acting clutch. The green neutral-indicator light goes out. You only buzz up to 20 mph in first, hardly thrilling, but shift up and feel the cam take over as the revs climb in second to 10,000 rpm. The large speedometer dial says 40 when you shift into third. Again the revs rise and you're doing 50 mph. Finally, in fourth the needle is flickering around 75 mph.

Sheer speed, of course, is not what the 160 is all about. Swopping cogs up and down as you sweep through a narrow, sharply curving stretch of blacktop is where the fun is. Averaging 40 mph can be exciting when warning signs and the behavior of automobile drivers say it's 30-mile-an-hour country.

The Super Sport has a curb weight of 288 pounds and feels even lighter as you lean it effortlessly around the sharpest turns. Brakes are wonderfully powerful without being grabby. You can pull the speed down instantly so long as you make full use of the racing-type front brake. When clamped on really hard, the rear brake is more effective than the 2.75 x 18 rear tire, which will slide. I'd like to see a 3.00 section tire on the rear, even if it slightly dulls the razor-sharp cornering.

The 160 has a lot of other endearing

features, some of which you miss on casual inspection. Gas consumption is in the ridiculous range—somewhere around 100 miles per gallon. With a 2.77 gallon tank this means you can buzz around locally for weeks without visiting a pump.

Night driving is as much fun as day driving because of the 30-watt headlight beam. Seating is unusually comfortable; the saddle, soft without being mushy, is narrow in front so you can grip the tank with your knees. There's plenty of room, and a grab strap, for a passenger. You can even adjust the stiffness of the rear suspension to any of three positions.

The little extras you might not ordinarily notice include a steering damper to adjust front and stiffness, knurled adjusters for clutch and brake cable, a gasoline filter, paper air filter, a plastic tube to vent the battery below the frame, oil filter, inspection plates that simplify practically every adjustment you're likely to make, and grease fittings all over. It's so overwhelming you would feel guilty unless you put 100,000 miles on the machine. All this attention to a mere 160! But that's why it's no ordinary 160.

Yamaha Big Bear Scrambler 250

About 15 years ago I stumbled onto the Adler 250, a remarkable two-stroke twin made in Germany. At that time such an engine was an oddity that aroused little popular interest or enthusiasm. Everyone *knew* what to expect from a two stroke. So I was surprised and delighted when the strange machine turned out to be a little bomb. That surprise and delight with two-stroke twins has never faded.

Choosing a current version of the design wasn't easy. Besides Yamaha, which has been a front runner among Japanese two strokes, there is Suzuki, Bridgestone, and Kawasaki. All make exciting twins in many sizes (the newest Suzuki is, of course, a whopping big 500 cc) and I would enjoy trying the whole bunch. What got the Big Bear the nod was its longevity —the model has been around getting its "bugs" squashed for several years. Add to that a time-proven oiling system, five-speed gearbox, and scrambler trim for clinchers.

With its upswept pipes and 3.6-gallon gas tank the YDS3C is a chubby rascal. And at 350 pounds it feels chubby. But once you get the mill popping with the left-side kickstarter (thank goodness she starts easily) you forget everything but the throttle and what it can do.

She has that light throttle feel when you

blast off in first. The engine stops four-stroking—an uncertain sound that's always distressed me—and buckles down to business. She quickly climbs up the rpm scale, topping out at about 25 mph. Back off on the gas and shift into second. This time when you feed her throttle the performance hits the cam. Those close-packed firing impulses rise in a powerful crescendo as the bike leaps ahead. You feel as though you're sitting on a miniature turbine engine that keeps accelerating with no apparent limit.

You hit 45 mph in second, shift into third and do it all over again with equal zest. This time she tops out at a little better than 60. Meanwhile, you discover, the handling is light and precise; she leans around curves easily and takes the bumpy road without fuss.

Now you're in fourth and though the response isn't quite as exciting as before you quickly reach 75 before running out of revs. Into fifth—which turns out to be like an overdrive—and you edge over the 80 mph mark.

Potent brakes are especially important on a fast two-stroke because you get little braking effect from the engine; most of it is from simple wind resistance. The Big Bear has big paws and clamping on both binders brings the speed down rapidly.

What makes the Big Bear Scrambler appealing is its big-bike feel and 28-hp engine. The tires are big by Japanese standards: 3.00 section in front and 3.50 in back. Battery ignition, three-position rear suspension, a 3.6-gallon gas tank, separate 0.4-gallon oil tank, a sturdy and easy-to-use sidestand, large speedometer dial, a tachometer, indicator lights for neutral and generator charging—it's all there.

Switching to knobby tires and removing the baffles in the mufflers (which adds another horsepower) converts her to a hot scrambles machine. Since my bike was in conventional road trim I couldn't try it on a dirt course. As a sporty road machine, however, she has that two-stroke twin feel, that special zing for moments when wringing maximum power and handling from a mediumweight is your kick. The fooler, I call it.

I'd like the YDS3C even better if the kickstarter were on the right side, the gearshift pedal a little wider, and the standard tires were knobbies. But when that engine winds these concerns fade.

BSA Victor Special 441

There was something masterful about the way trials, enduro, and even scrambles riders used to blast through the roughest going with perfect control on 500 cc four-stroke singles. It wasn't just the blasting part, it was also the slow plonking with instant torque ready to pull them out of the jaws of disaster when all seemed lost. I grew to admire the big thumpers and secretly coveted one. But most were heavy and looked uncomfortable—not the kind of machinery I wanted to wrestle through mud, over rocks, and across stream beds.

That was many years ago, and as vertical twins and the new breed of two strokes grabbed the spotlight those stalwart thumpers became virtually extinct. Then along came the BSA Victor Special, which reportedly did all those wonderful

things without the penalties of overweight and discomfort. Since 34 horsepower propelled only 300 pounds and the bike had all the off-road features the British know

YAMAHA BIG BEAR SCRAMBLER
Engine Type: Two stroke, twin cylinder
Displacement: 246 cc
Bore and stroke: 56 x 50 mm
Horsepower @ rpm:
28 @ 8,000 rpm—muffler baffles out
21 @ 7,500 rpm—muffler baffles in
Compression Ratio: 7.8 : 1
Ignition: Battery   Top Speed: 80 mph
Number of Speeds: Five
Miles per gallon: 40   Weight: 350 lbs.
Tires: Front—3.00x18   Rear—3.50x18
Price: $659 f.o.b. Philadelphia, Pa.

YAMAHA BIG BEAR SCRAMBLER

BSA VICTOR SPECIAL

so well how to provide, I decided this was what I'd wanted for so long.

It was. Despite the sacrilege of road tires, the Victor looked like the very model of a no-nonsense competition mount. The detachable headlight, upraised alloy front and rear fenders, high-flow exhaust with stubby muffler tucked inside the frame, skid plate, rubber-mounted speedometer with trip meter and squat gas tank all added up that way.

Once I got her thumping—not easy work on any big single—it became clear that the Victor had the other competition features too. First I took her out on the road to see what she had in the engine room. In

BSA VICTOR SPECIAL
Engine type: Four stroke,
single cylinder, OHV
Displacement: 441 cc.
Bore and stroke: 79 x 90 mm.
Horsepower @ rpm: 34 @ 6,000 (est.)
Compression Ratio: 9.4 : 1
Ignition: Battery   Top Speed: 90 mph
Number of speeds: Four
Miles per gallon: 50
Weight: 300 lbs.
Tires: Front—3.25x19   Rear—4.00x18
Price: $930 f.o.b. Nutley, N.J.

first gear she thumped right up to 30 mph; then I shifted into second and pushed the needle up to 50. Vibration by now was making the speedometer needle hard to read. Then into third gear and up the rpm scale again, this time to 65 mph. Finally, in fourth, she was still picking up speed gradually at 80 when I ran out of road.

In the rough the Victor seemed more at home. Standing on the foot pegs, I puttered over to a short, steep hill in first gear. A tweak of the spring-loaded throttle and she walked up without hesitation. At the top I lifted the shift lever up into second gear by rocking my foot backward on the right footpeg, still standing up. Another tweak of the light-acting throttle and the Victor jumped ahead. I rode around for some time, still standing on the pegs, shift-ing up and down effortlessly until I took the Victor's tractor-like torque for granted.

What surprised me was the light feel and remarkable maneuverability of the bike at

BMW R60 & SIDECAR

BMW R60 & SIDECAR
Engine type: Four stroke, twin cylinder, OHV
Displacement: 593 cc
Bore and stroke: 72 x 73 mm.
Horsepower @ rpm: 30 @ 5,800
Compression ratio: 7.5 : 1
Ignition: Magneto Top speed: 65 mph
Number of speeds: Four
Miles per gallon: 36 Weight: 705 lbs.
Tires: Front—4.00x18 Rear—4.00x18
Sidecar—4.00x18 Price: $2,079

low speed. It's nicely balanced, though a little light in the nose if you pour on the coal; "wheelies" are not only easy, they can be a nuisance. Handlebars are relatively flat and narrow, so that your arms are in a direct line with your shoulders. The range of movement is extraordinary—you can turn the wheel either way to what seems like a right angle, though this is obviously an exaggeration. If you didn't know better you'd swear you were handling a 250, except for the engine. A great feeling.

The brakes are excellent, especially the rear one, which can readily be locked tight by pressing on the large pedal—a necessity for sliding down steep dirt hills. The front brake, apparently for safety reasons, is not as powerful as you would expect on a machine of this size. It's not possible to lock the front wheel under ordinary conditions, and maybe this is just as well.

There are some excellent touches: a really practical side stand, finger-operated adjusters for clutch and front brake, narrow saddle and tank so you can get a good knee grip, rear sprocket bolted to the brake drum for quick sprocket changes, and a low-enough seating position so you can put both feet on the ground despite a hefty eight-inch ground clearance.

I'd like the thumper even better if she were easier to start, came with knobby tires as standard equipment, a slightly wider shift pedal, and a slightly lower overall gearing (larger rear sprocket). Then she'd be perfect for trials and enduros. You can file that under lily-gilding.

BMW R-60 and Hollandia Sidecar

Over the years I've tested the whole line of BMWs, from the now defunct 250 cc single to the hot R69S. Quality, smoothness, and flexibility have always been hallmarks of the German-made machines. These qualities, as well as three unique BMW features, make the 600 cc twins especially suitable for sidecar use. The three unique features are the horizontally opposed cylinders for a low center of gravity, the shaft drive to handle a greater load without adjustment or breakage, and Earles-type front forks that can be adjusted for trail.

The BMW R-60 and Hollandia sidecar outfit is described in detail in the next chapter, "Fun on Three Wheels."

Triumph Trophy Sports 650

For several years my wife and I rode one of the first Triumph Thunderbirds imported into this country as a solo machine.

Then we switched sprockets and drove a few more years as a sidecar outfit. At a time when most heavyweights were either 500 cc or 74-cubic-inch machines, the 650 vertical twin from England was an oddity. Its sprung-hub rear wheel was another oddity.

Since then the Triumph's engine and gearbox have been combined into a single unit, the sprung hub has given way to the now-common swinging-arm rear suspension, front suspension and steering have been substantially improved, the brakes have had their potency increased, and the electrics are more effective and reliable. One thing has remained practically unchanged: that deep-throated exhaust note. It's like a signature that identifies Triumph over the years.

Choosing the Trophy Sports (TR6R) rather than the hotter Bonneville (T120R) was not an oversight. The Bonneville's second carburetor adds seven more horsepower, giving it 52. This puts it in the racing class at a sacrifice in tractability, gas mileage, and reliability. What I wanted was a modernized Thunderbird, a gently stressed bike for fast medium-distance riding—especially with the added burden of a passenger. With its 3½-gallon gas tank and modest consumption the Trophy Sports is such a tourer.

Climbing back on a Triumph was like old home week. She started right up with a few prods of the very effective kickstarter, which produced that familiar throaty roar—not a raucous noise but a very authoritative and reassuring one. I pressed the shift lever down into first and felt the same short, crisp movement. A smooth, progressive clutch took up the load and away we went with what seemed like considerably more zip than my old Thunderbird, even with sidecar gearing. In a trice I was charging along at 45 mph. Upshifting into second produced another stomach-unsettling speed increase, to 65. Third boosted the machine to 85 before I ran out of road. The bike has been clocked at 103 mph in fourth, which is much faster than I would ever drive it. What interests me more is a 0 to 60 acceleration figure of six seconds, a very impressive performance for a standard road bike.

Performance, of course, is what I wanted the Triumph for. She will keep you ahead of or get you away from most cars with ease. In fact I discovered that I was reading the tachometer (a big-dialed beauty) instead of the speedometer. I read the "40" as 40 mph instead of 4,000 rpm. Seemed like a fairly swift 40 mph but not markedly so. When I realized the goof and glanced at the adjoining instrument it showed 60 mph. So much for high-performance engines and deceptive tachometers (which should all have single digits from one to nine thousand revolutions).

Brakes are now really up to the engine's capability. A new twin-leading-shoe front brake (full-width, eight inch) brings down the speed as quickly as it goes up, helped by a potent rear brake. Besides the handsome tachometer there's a matching speedometer with trip odometer, easily reset by a knurled shaft sticking out the side of the instrument. The ammeter is a welcome addition to the group of instruments. There's a green neutral light too, but it's hard to tell when it's on; perhaps a brighter bulb would help.

Much as I enjoyed the Trophy Sports' handsome looks (except for the garish disc on the left side of the front wheel) sizzling performance, powerful brakes, and fine handling, I'd like it even better if the seating were more comfortable. A seat height of 31 inches makes it difficult for short-legged riders like me to get a foot com-

TRIUMPH TROPHY SPORTS
Engine type: Four stroke, twin cylinder, OHV
Displacement: 649 cc.
Bore and stroke: 71 x 82 mm.
Horsepower @ rpm: 45 @ 6,500
Compression ratio: 9:1
Ignition: Battery   Top Speed: 103 mph
Number of speeds: Four
Miles per gallon: n.a.
Weight: 386 pounds
Tires: Front—3.25x19   Rear—4.00x18
Price: $1,280 f.o.b. Baltimore

TRIUMPH TROPHY SPORTS

41

fortably on the ground. The handlebars are wide and rubber-mounted, which means wide-stretched arms and a slightly wobbly feel to the bars. The seat is attractive-looking, with its "pleated" ridges, but forces you to sit in one place, which is farther back than I like.

These personal preferences can, of course, be taken care of without affecting the really important Triumph Trophy Sports features. And it would be worth the effort.

Harley-Davidson Sportster 883

When you're feeling hairy-chested and competitive to the eyeballs there's nothing like an XLCH, the 883 cc magneto-ignition Harley Davidson. I rode one of the first Sportsters some years ago and remember being impressed both with the machine's performance and with Harley-Davidson's good sense.

At the time, the British 650s were cut-

HARLEY-DAVIDSON SPORTSTER XLCH	
Engine type: Four stroke, twin cylinder, OHV	
Displacement: 883 cc.	
Bore and stroke: 76.2 x 96.8 mm.	
Horsepower @ rpm: 58 @ 6,800	
Compression ratio: 9.0 : 1	
Ignition: Magneto	
Top Speed: 115 mph	
Number of speeds: Four	
Miles per gallon: n.a.	
Weight: 460 lbs.	
Tires: Front — 3.50x19	Rear — 4.00x18
Price: $1,650 f.o.b. Milwaukee	

HARLEY-DAVIDSON SPORTSTER XLCH

ting into the new crop of riders who would normally have bought the 74-cubic-inch Harley-Davidson, for lack of a choice. To bring out a big V twin in a relatively light pivoting-fork frame without massive fenders was an act of genius. It was even better than a bobbed (stripped) 74.

For a rider like me who started out on an Indian Chief (since gone to the happy hunting ground) and then switched over to a smaller British bike, the Sportster is the best of both worlds. Technically the V twin may not be ideal, with its uneven firing impulses, tall engine, and masked rear cylinder. But there *is* no substitute for displacement, and the Sportster has raw power at low rpms. Add to this the handling of a smaller bike—brakes, suspension, weight distribution—and you have a compelling combination.

The best accessory for the magneto-fired XLCH is a long hill to roll it down. My right thigh got well-bruised from banging against the top of a rear suspension unit before I applied this useful trick. But once the bike barked into life it became clear that the Sportster really *is* all engine.

I snicked the short shift lever down into first with a light push and let out the robust multiplate dry clutch. She took hold smoothly and we began to pick up speed with the invincibility of a locomotive. Acceleration is always a stomach-tingling experience, but it's even more exciting when you sense a considerable weight being set in motion. (Opening and closing the Sportster's throttle while in first gear will demonstrate what I mean.)

Without really trying we topped 45 mph in first. A lift of the shift lever into second, another application of the wick, and we zoomed up to 65. The same in third: 85. This is all local highways will stand, so I never wound out in fourth. But the XLCH has been clocked at 115 mph and considering a 58-horsepower output I have no reason to doubt it.

All that power makes the Sportster fine for local travel, too, where cruising speeds average 35 mph—you burble along easily in third gear, or even fourth, and blast ahead without shifting down whenever road conditions warrant. Or if you're in a hurry to leave someone behind as a traffic light turns green you can reach 60 mph in six seconds and cover the first quarter-of-a-mile in about 14. Makes that hair on your chest stand right out. Torque, by the way, is a remarkable 52 lb./ft.

But what I like the lean giant for is its high-speed, long-distance touring capa-bility. A machine that can top out at 115 mph can hold 75 hour after hour without working up an expensive sweat. Fortunately the saddle and riding position are comfortable too. Brakes are excellent—the front one has recently been improved. Handling, once you get over an initial fright at the Sportster's powerful thrust, is good for such a large machine. Its long wheelbase, 3.50x19 and 4.00x18 tires, 460 pounds, and heavy-duty suspension make the Sportster better for the long straights and gentle curves of expressways, however.

One great thing the Harley-Davidson has—it's almost a Milwaukee trade-mark —is the wonderfully loud horn. Add to that a neatly paired tachometer and speed-ometer, a handy ignition "kill" button, oil and generator signal lights, and a 90-watt 12-volt generator.

I'd like the lean giant even more with the larger (4.0 gallon) gas tank; 2.2 gallons doesn't go far on the turnpike. More effective mufflers or at least a longer pipe from the front cylinder that carries its explosions further aft would be welcome. Easier starting, larger speedometer-dial numbers, and a shorter throw to the shift lever round out the suggestions. Either way, just try to pry my hand loose from that throttle!

Acknowledgments

Lacking the $7,626 f.o.b. price of these seven machines, assembling my dream stable would have been impossible without the generous help of distributors and dealers. The Hondas were provided with the blessings of American Honda Motor Company and Honda of Mineola in Mineola, New York. Yamaha's Big Bear Scrambler came from Queens Scooter Corp. of New York City. The BSA Victor Special was loaned by BSA, Inc., of Nutley, N.J. BMW R-60 and Hollandia sidecar outfit came from East Coast Cycles of Yonkers, N.Y., with the assistance of Butler & Smith, Inc., of New York City. Triumph's Trophy Sports was provided by The Triumph Corp. of Baltimore, Md., through Sagan's of Uniondale, N.Y., and the Harley-Davidson Sportster was loaned by Pfaff Harley-Davidson Sales Co. of Lynbrook, N.Y.

We lucky motorcycle writers and editors would have to pack up our typewriters and go out of business without the help of distributors and dealers like these who entrust us with their precious stock in trade. Yet they seldom get credit, much less thanks. For once, here's the credit—and the thanks.

Sidecar racing, which has never diminished in popularity in Europe, is catching on again in Canada and the U.S. This far-out pair, making a sharp turn on a BMW outfit, won recently at a Mosport, Canada, race.

Fun on Three Wheels

WHY SHOULD anyone want to hang a third wheel on a perfectly good motorcycle? A sidecar outfit costs as much as a small car, requires special driving talents, has a much lower top speed than a solo, takes up more space on the road and in the garage, uses more gas, and wears out engine and tires faster.

Until you've driven one for a while you'll never fully appreciate the appeal of a sidecar. It's completely different from a solo machine because, like a car, it can't lean to change direction. Unlike a car it's largely steered with the throttle and, when the handlebar is cocked sharply, can practically move sideways at highway speeds or turn in its own length at a walking pace.

There are some good excuses for driving an outfit, of course. They're unusual and many are downright beautiful. You can pack your wife or girl friend into the hack in her regular clothes and stow luggage in the trunk besides. A small child can even sit in her lap. Snow, rain, ice, loose gravel have little effect on the stability of an outfit—the British have long considered them the safest of all road vehicles. Being considerably wider than a solo bike they're more easily seen—and

respected—by our enemies the car drivers. You can also do kooky things with them, as some of the photos show.

Your maiden voyage at the helm of a sidecar outfit takes a hero's courage and, for the safety of humanity, should be made in the middle of an empty one-acre parking lot. Let's assume it's a properly set-up rig like the BMW R-60 and Hollandia sidecar (generously loaned to us by East Coast Cycle of Yonkers, N. Y.). As the sketches show, this means a slight toe-in of the sidecar wheel and a slight lean-out of the bike.

With the bike in first gear you slip in the clutch and give the throttle a hearty twist. (There's nothing subtle about a sidecar outfit, you exaggerate everything to make up for the clumsiness and extra weight—more throttle, more thrust on the handlebars, a heavier hand and foot on the brakes.) The bike charges forward, circling automatically to the right.

It's your first experience with a double-track vehicle that has only one powered wheel and it's a shock. The bike's rear wheel, of course, is trying to pivot the motorcycle around the sidecar. And it would succeed except for two things: the

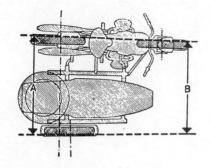

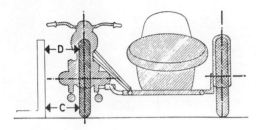

In lining up the outfit, at top, the sidecar wheel should toe-in slightly so that the distance B is 1.2 to 1.6 inches less than distance A. With the driver and sidecar passenger in place, the motorcycle should lean out so that D, in the bottom drawing, is $\frac{3}{8}$ to $\frac{7}{16}$ of an inch less than distance C.

Passenger sits low in sidecar, well-protected from wind by plastic windshield. The R-60 and Hollandia sidehack can creep along or hit 65 mph on highway.

sidecar wheel starts to turn and you cock the handlebars firmly to the left, pushing on one and pulling on the other.

Now the bike straightens out on a proper course as she picks up speed. The torque and exhaust note suggest a V-8 powerplant —overall gearing has been substantially lowered to handle the heavier load. You shut off the gas to shift into second and make another big discovery: the outfit slows down immediately. So you shift quickly into second. (Quick shifting soon becomes a habit as you discover the importance of keeping power on for control.) Second is a great gear on every outfit because it's got zoooom—plenty of torque with a respectable top speed.

By this time you're at the edge of the field and make the third big discovery. You roll back the throttle and the machine falls off to the left like a sailboat that's lost its wind. But the outfit has too much momentum to stop without help. Having to clamp on binders while the three-wheeler is heading off course toward disaster can churn your digestive juices something shameful.

Four appendages hardly seem enough. Both arms are twisting the handlebars to compensate for the leftward drift, the right hand is squeezing the front brake lever, the left hand is squeezing the clutch. Meanwhile your right foot is tromping on the rear brake pedal and the left is shifting down into neutral. Small wonder so many beginning sidecar drivers end up in a fence, hedge, or sand bank before they figure out what to do. The only thing you don't have to worry about is falling off the machine, a small but welcome favor.

In the course of time you've made a dozen runs back and forth across the field. On the last ones you've even been quick enough to get into third gear briefly before running out of space. Stops have become smooth and self-assured; you've got the outfit under control all the time. Now let's try some figure eights and see how you do. Play it safe, make 'em big.

You let in the clutch, twist the throttle,

Rear view of the BMW rig shows the spacious passenger compartment and the trunk in back of seat. Black sidecar has been pin-striped to match bike.

and start a circle to the right by not correcting the outfit's natural tendency to take off in that direction. A quick up-shift into second, you gun the engine and in seconds reach the widest point of the lower loop. Back off on the throttle, the outfit falls off to the left; you help a little with the handlebars.

On a straight course once more, you feed it gas again and soon reach the end of the diagonal in the figure eight—the right-hand loop at the top is just ahead. It's your first right-hander at speed and you're uncertain what to do. Should you give it more gas to help pivot the machine around the sidecar? Or keep the throttle where it is and cock the wheel to the right? If you back off on the gas the outfit will drift leftward—just the opposite of what you want.

Cranking on more throttle appeals to youre ego, but the coward center in your stomach says "no." Instead you cock the handlebar to the right and instantly the sidecar wheel lifts off the ground. Panic! You back off on the gas, straighten the bars, and lean toward the hack to push it down.

It doesn't make sense. Why should the *inside* wheel lift; it seems that turning toward the hack should push that third wheel down. You're a victim of physics, centrifugal force to be exact. On a right-hand turn the bike is on the circumference of an imaginary circle, with the sidecar nearer its center. Just as water pushes

against the bottom of a bucket that's whirling around your head, the sidecar tries to join the bike. The result is a shift in the outfit's center of gravity away from the sidecar wheel toward the machine, causing the sidecar to lighten and lift.

On a left-hander, of course, centrifugal force shifts the center of gravity toward the hack and you zip around with impunity because the bike, with you on it, is more than heavy enough to stay down. But it's not impossible to lift a small bike on a fast left-hand bend with a heavy passenger in the sidecar!

Now that you know about centrifugal force you try again and again. Gradually you learn how fast and how sharply you can take a right-hander. You even stow a 100-pound sack of cement on the floor of the sidecar when there's no passenger to hold it down. The trick, you discover, is to back off part way on the throttle and clamp on the binders just before the bend to slow the outfit down. Then you cock the wheel to the right, give 'er some gas to pivot around, and lean low over the sidecar. Once around the curve you pour on the coals, straighten up on the saddle, and hold the wheel on a straight course. Acrobatic? It doesn't have to be, but that's half the fun.

A Ride in the BMW Outfit

Now that you're a pro, off the road at least, let's take a ride in the borrowed BMW R-60 and Hollandia sidecar. The flat-twin 600cc machine is ideal for sidecar use—as many decades of BMW dominance in continental European sidecar racing prove. With its outstretched cylinders the BMW has an ideally low center of gravity. The Hollandia is a spacious single-seater with lift-up windshield and a trunk.

Climb into the hack and I'll give you a fast ride over narrow, twisty roads on Long Island's hilly north shore. By standing on the right footpeg and holding onto the handlebars I can give the transverse kickstart pedal a shove without getting off the machine. Starting is easier with a sidecar—it's always upright. The BMW growls into life, a click down into first, let out the clutch and the bike starts to creep forward gradually. The heavy-duty single-plate clutch is just what's needed for an outfit.

We take off briskly and she winds up to 20 mph in bottom gear. I shift quickly just before the first right-hand bend and she zooms ahead, sweeping around the curve as I hunch over against the sidehack, right foot standing on the sidecar fitting, left foot across the saddle. Safely around now, we're doing 35 mph in second. It's a downhill straight with a sharp lefthander at the bottom. Into third and we swoop down the hill wide open doing 50. The outfit feels steady as a rock as we approach the bend. Back off on the throttle, a touch of the binders, I lean out to the left and she wheels around the bend.

Now we're on a long, level straight with plenty of room to open up. Into fourth, bring her up to full throttle again. She's doing 65 mph and it feels like 80. That's another kick to side-carring—you don't have to go very fast to feel as though you're flying.

Soon we're off the level concrete and into a winding stretch of two-lane, high-crowned macadam. Here's where the fun really begins. Average speed through this section is 35 mph on a solo. Dropping into third gives just the right combination of torque and speed. There's no one coming so we'll use the full road width.

We dive from the middle of the road into

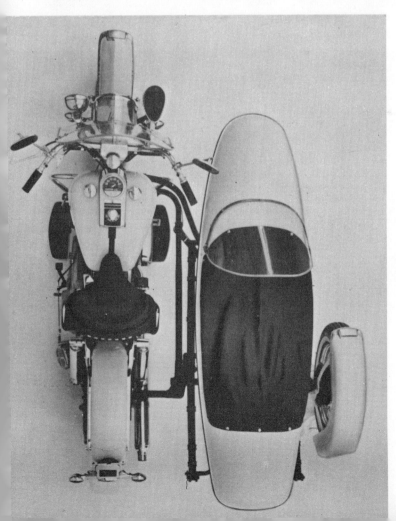

Harley-Davidson outfit consists of the Electra Glide and the new glass-fiber sidecar. Tonneau cover, used to keep rain out, hides passenger seat.

The Harley-Davidson sidecar has full leaf-spring suspension and hydraulically operated brake. Tubular chassis is bolted to motorcycle at 3 points.

The Jawa 360 and Velorex sidecar is the smallest outfit offered as a unit. Motorcycle is a 350 cc two-stroke twin. The sidecar is glass fiber.

Credit: Photo courtesy of "Motorcyclist"

a right-hand bend, cutting in so close that the sidecar wheel bounces along the uneven shoulder, shaking the whole outfit. I'm leaning far over to the right, my head almost on the sidecar passenger's shoulder. Give her the gun coming out, we're crossing the road diagonally, heading for the apex of a sharp left-hander. I move back across the saddle, leaning far out to the left and cocking the wheel that way. Then back off on the gas and we shoot around the curve, straightening out when we're in the middle of the road again.

Sounds crazy, perhaps, but that's the big kick. It's driving close to the limit, sizing up a corner split seconds before you get there, controlling both speed and sideways drift largely with the throttle, wrestling with the handlebars on tight turns, throwing your weight around to counteract centrifugal force. You're as busy as a one-man band and if you stay at it for a while you have a physique like King Kong and a quiet pride in having mastered a rare and demanding skill.

The rest is more of the same, so let's go back home and talk about some of the fine points and about the different rigs available.

Close-up of the BMW Outfit

Gearing on the R-60 is perfect for sidecar use. They've lowered the rear-end ratio from 3.18 to 3.86 to increase torque in all four gears. Then they've lowered and widened the ratios for first, second, and third. First is 5.33 instead of 4.71, second is 3.02 instead of 2.72, third is 2.04 instead of 1.94, and fourth remains 1.54.

Shifting, considered somewhat heavy by some for solo riding, has just the right feel for sidecar use. With that extra weight to pull and the higher revs, you want a positive feel and the BMW has it. I never missed a gear change or felt the clutch slip.

Front and rear suspension are modified for sidecar use. On the front end stiffer springs are fitted, shock absorber travel is reduced to match the heavier springs, and the swinging-arm pivot bearing on the Earles-type fork is shifted to the front position. Shifting the pivot bearing, a unique advantage of this fork, reduces the trail and improves steering. It really works, I discovered: At a steady 40 mph the outfit kept a straight course with no hands on the bars. This is also a tribute to the steering damper and the careful alignment of the outfit, of course. All the rear suspension takes is stiffer springs.

Ideally, a sidecar outfit should have a brake in the sidecar wheel, coupled by rod, cable, or hydraulic oil line to the rear brake of the motorcycle. This gives the added safety of three-wheel braking—more braking effect to match the greater weight and a retarding effect on the sidecar wheel to counter its tendency to swing the outfit to the left on high-speed panic stops. Actually, though the Hollandia sidecar wheel had no brake—and none is available from the maker—the R-60's two potent binders were perfectly adequate for the 100 miles or so of local and expressway traveling I did with it. The outfit's modest weight—only 705 pounds for R-60 and hack—helps in the stopping department.

A sidecar-wheel brake is desirable none-theless, especially if you carry a heavy passenger and piles of luggage. It needs to be coupled in such a way that the bike's rear brake takes hold first, followed a second or so later by the sidecar-wheel brake as you push down harder on the pedal. This stops the outfit in a straight line instead of causing it to swerve to the right under hard braking.

With a sidecar outfit it's especially important to use the front-wheel brake to the fullest. This not only spreads the work and brake-lining and tire wear, it stops the outfit quicker. Fortunately it's perfectly safe to clamp the front brake on hard because you're holding the bars steady and the outfit can't fall over. Here the BMW has it all over the Indian 74 I used to drive. The BMW front brake is a powerful decelerator while the Indian front brake could barely keep the outfit from rolling downhill under the influence of gravity.

Speaking of gravity, it can be a strenuous pain to heave a sidecar rig around even on the level, much less uphill. Yet without a reverse gear this is hard to avoid completely. You learn to avoid situations where pushing will be necessary if your outfit has no reverse gear. Luckily they turn sharply.

No reverse gear is available on BMW, but most drivers of light and medium-weight outfits manage well enough without them. If given the choice of losing one of their four forward speeds for a reverse they'd probably elect the four forward speeds. You get lots of use out of the forward speeds and only occasional use out of the reverse.

Most motorcycles have just enough generator output to handle the normal lighting load of a solo machine, but not enough reserve capacity to handle extra sidecar lights. The BMW is no exception. Its Bosch generator puts out 60 watts, of which 50 are used steadily by regular solo lighting. Stoplight and turn signal use 18 watts each, intermittently, which means you're overdrawn at the battery by 26 watts every time you make a turn. With an eight ampere-hour battery it doesn't take long to exhaust all credit.

On the test BMW outfit there was an added steady drain of 10 watts (for running light and tail light) and another 18 intermittent watts for the second stop light. Transferring the right-hand turn signal from the handlebar to the sidecar fender, of course, has no effect on the accounting.

A tinge of red around the edge of the generator warning light confirms the arith-

Flight sidecar is a lightweight hack attached here to a Triumph TR-6. It comes without a sidecar wheel brake. Sells for $415 f.o.b., Bolyston, Mass.

Monza comes in three models, with and without a brake, and available in de luxe trim. Convertible top is standard and machine is a Velocette.

metic: the full 60 watt output of the generator gets used up by the lights on a sidecar rig. The solution is to put an automobile battery in the sidecar trunk and charge it occasionally when a lot of night driving pulls out more juice than goes in.

The BMW has two other things going for it as a sidecar power unit. One is the flexibility of its engine. You have to shift enough even with a big-displacement engine, so what you *don't* want is a fussy, highly tuned bike that must stay within a narrow rpm range to crank out its power. The BMW R-60 has a broad power band that lets it run comfortably over a wide speed range in each gear.

Try to imagine someone steering a sidecar outfit with ape hangers and you'll anticipate the BMW's other asset. It has wide, flat handlebars that give plenty of mechanical advantage when you're twisting the front wheel. Minor? Not if you take a long trip.

Some sidecar enthusiasts have hitched hacks to the BMW R-69S because it develops 42 horsepower to the R-60's 30. The extra 12 hp come from higher rpm—

7,000 instead of 5,800—and a compression ratio of 9.5 instead of 7.5 to 1. Both have 600cc displacements, of course. It's possible to get a lower rear-end ratio for the R-69S, but not different gearbox ratios. The hydraulic steering damper fitted as standard on the R-69S is unsuitable for sidecar use and a mechanical damper, standard on the R-60, is recommended.

Whether the R-69S makes a better sidecar machine than the R-60 is an open question. On the affirmative side, Ted Penton and Bill Cleaver hold the coast-to-coast sidecar record of a little over 60 hours from New York to Los Angeles with an R-69S and BMW sidehack (BMW no longer makes sidecars, incidentally).

The R-60 in sidecar trim has an f.o.b. New York price tag of $1,364. The Hollandia sidecar adds $680 and the sidecar fittings cost another $35. This totals $2,079 and does not include transportation, sales taxes, or set-up charges.

Harley-Davidson Electra Glide Outfit

As the biggest, most powerful production motorcycle in the world, the Electra

Monaco is a large single-seater with hinged deck and squared-off trunk. Extra luggage can be strapped to trunk lid. Bike is a Triumph Bonneville.

Palma is a two-seater Watsonian. Adult sits up forward, a child up to six years can sit behind. The sidecar sells for $545 f.o.b. Machine is BMW R-69.

Glide is a natural choice to power a side-hack. Coincidentally, Harley-Davidson—which has always made its own sidecars—has just come out with a completely new one made of fiberglass instead of sheet metal.

The Electra Glide also comes in two states of tune: the FL model with 55 hp and the FLH with 60 hp, both at 5,400. The difference is mainly due to compression ratio: the FL has a 7.25 to 1 ratio and the FLH has an 8 to 1 ratio. Either model has enough zip to cruise a sidecar outfit loaded to the gunwales at expressway speeds all day. Considering the bike alone has a curb weight of 783 pounds, these power outputs are not disproportionate, however.

Some of the Electra Glide's automotive-type features, which might seem out of character for a solo motorcycle, fit in nicely with a sidecar outfit. Tires are 5.00 x 16 monsters that give plenty of braking area, lots of wear, and a soft ride. The rear brake is hydraulic, which means the sidecar-wheel brake can be hydraulically operated too, through an oil line from the master brake cylinder. (The Electra Glide's

front brake is a hill holder like the one on my old Indian.) The standard electric starter makes even more sense on a sidecar outfit, where leaping around on a kick-starter pedal is made more hazardous by sidecar connections.

The Electra Glide's larger scale is an asset for sidecar use. Its greater weight, longer wheelbase make it more stable and comfortable. Automotive-type engine design and parts provide the extra durability an outfit should have. The dry multiple-disc clutch can handle 248 lb./ft. of torque (the FLH engine develops 65 lb./ft. at 3,200 rpm).

Electrics are no problem on the Electra Glide. Its 12-volt D.C. generator puts out 120 watts for starter, ignition, and lights. Once under way in solo trim, the machine draws only 64 watts steadily for lights. Flashing both stop light and turn signals adds another 64 watts intermittently. The sidehack draws an extra eight watts for running and tail light, while a second stop light would add 32 watts intermittently. Thus, total steady drain would be 72 watts and total intermittent drain 168 watts.

Despite this occasional deficit of 48 watts, the over-sized standard battery is probably adequate for most night driving.

An Electra Glide in sidecar trim has heavier suspension springs, a solo saddle (more comfortable than the buddy seat), and sidecar gearing. Overall gearing is lowered by substituting a 19-tooth engine sprocket for a 23-tooth one on the FL and changing to a 21-tooth sprocket from a 24 on the FLH.

The three forward speeds are spread widely in an attempt to cover the same range as the four speeds in the solo models. The FLH, with its greater horsepower and torque, comes closer to succeeding than the FL—all of its ratios are higher and top speed falls about halfway between the third and fourth speeds of the solo model. Reverse gears have about the same ratios as first.

The f.o.b. Milwaukee price of an FL without any options is $1,735. The sidecar, also without options, is $410. A windshield for the sidecar adds $13, sidecar connections $59. This totals $2,217 excluding transportation, taxes, and set-up charges. If you want a reverse gear it's $13 more.

Jawa 360 Sidecar Outfit

The smallest rig available as a single unit from one source is the Jawa 350 cc two-stroke twin with Velorex sidecar. The four-speed bike turns up 21 hp at 5,000 rpm and is capable of 75 mph in solo form. As supplied for sidecar use it has 16-inch wheels.

The sidecar has a tubular frame and glass fiber body. Suspension is by rubber blocks and bushings plus a telescopic shock absorber. A sidecar brake coupled to the rear-brake pedal is included, along with an acrylic plastic windshield, foam cushions, and a lockable compartment behind the backrest. The fender has running lights front and rear and can be raised on a hinge to expose the sidecar wheel. The sidehack weighs 154 lbs. and has a rated carrying capacity of 231 lbs. for passenger and luggage.

Fittings are supplied for attachment to the Jawa 250 and 350 cc models, but are "easily modified for attachment to other makes of motorcycles," according to the importer.

Without testing this rig on the road, which could not be arranged in time, it's difficult to guess how it performs. No mention is made of special sidecar gearing or suspension, though a smaller engine sprocket is undoubtedly available. An educated guess is that with such lower overall gearing the outfit would hum along contentedly at 45-50 mph on the level. Given normal Jawa reliability, the bike would probably stand up reasonably well in such heavy-duty service. With the additional sidecar-fender lights drawing only another 3-4 watts each, the generator would probably not be overworked. However, this 350 does not appear to have a battery, which could be a serious handicap if extensive stop-and-go night driving is planned. Without a battery the bright-

The Kenilworth two-seater saloon holds two full-sized adults. Waterproof canvas top can be rolled back. Frame is made of plywood, panels of steel.

Norman Grabowski, Hollywood actor, owns this way-out sidecar rig. The machine is a six-cylinder Corvair engine mounted in a 1941 military Indian frame. German Steib sidecar chassis, above and right, carries a glass-fiber body adapted from a "T" roadster body. It was specially upholstered.

ness of the outfit's lights depend on engine revolutions—a nerve-wracking circumstance.

Watsonian Sidecars

If you already have a suitable machine and want just a sidehack to hang on it, Randy Wilson of Boylston, Mass., may have the answer. He imports Watsonian rigs from Birmingham, England, where they've been made for over 50 years. Watsonian makes a dozen models ranging from light-weight sports jobs to big two-seaters with permanent roofs. The photos give an idea of the types and prices, which range from $415 to $545 f.o.b. Boylston.

You can even buy a bare chassis and build your own hack. The Light Velvet chassis, used on the Flight sidecar, sells for $225; the Mark IV Heavy Duty chassis is $260.

Fittings are the crucial aspect of adding a sidecar. Without the right ones you either fail completely or create an abomination that won't handle safely, much less comfortably. Even suitable fittings are worthless, of course, in amateur hands. It's always possible to experiment if you're sure you have the right fittings, but be prepared to spend many hours at it. And head for the middle of that empty parking lot when you try out each adjustment. An easier, and safer, route is to find a dealer who has had experience with sidecars. Or if you're not too far from Boylston, Mass., you can drive over and have Randy hook up the hack himself. The charge is $20. It may be a bit harrowing to learn to handle an outfit while you're driving home through traffic, however.

Sidecars with fittings for Triumph 650 cc twins from 1963 to the present are available in stock. So are hacks for single and twin-cylinder BMWs. If you have a unit-construction BSA twin, Norton twin, Matchless twin, Panther single, Velocette twin, Honda 450, Royal Enfield 750 cc twin, or a Harley-Davidson XLH you can order a sidecar with the proper fittings. These special orders take six to eight weeks for delivery and require a $50 deposit.

Included in the price is a convertible top, storage space behind the seat, and a choice of colors. You can have all black, black and white, black and silver, all white, or the same color as your bike.

The British hitch up lightweights like the Flight to machines as small as 250 cc. This may be all right for around-town use. But for highway use, which means trips of any length, you will quickly lose your enthusiasm for sidecarring with anything smaller than the 450 Honda. There is no substitute for displacement when it comes to hauling a sidecar. Even with a hefty engine you should gear down and beef up the suspension. The extra weight of a sidecar bears down heavily on the front end and without heavier springs you will probably bottom on every bump and pothole. It's not impossible to break fork springs and wear out seals.

If you have the idea that driving the outfit would be fun on Monday, Wednesday, and Friday while riding the bike solo would be fun Tuesday, Thursday, and Saturday don't fool yourself. It's not that easy to take an outfit apart and put it back together. Riding solo all summer and with a sidecar all winter would make sense though. So would having one machine for solo use and another—perhaps the same or an older model—set up for sidecar use.

But however you manage it, once you join the club you'll be hooked. Who knows, one of motorcycling's oldest variations may come back strong again.

The only production side-valve engine unit is 200 cc opposed-twin water-cooled Velocette.

What's Ahead in Motorcycle Design

By J. B. Nicholson

J. B. Nicholson is a motorcycle distributor of long experience in Saskatoon, Canada, and an expert on motorcycle repair. His well-known book Modern Motorcycle Mechanics, *first published in 1942, is now in its fifth edition.*

IN NO PERIOD of motorcycle history have there been developments that have so expanded motorcycle interest and popularity comparable with those of the 1960s. The Honda story alone is without parallel. The most significant motor developments have been the high-rpm capabilities of the small-displacement overhead-valve and overhead-camshaft Honda engines. And, paralleling the Honda achievements in the four-stroke field are the vast improvements in two-stroke engine technology by a variety of Japanese manufacturers, notably Suzuki, Yamaha and Kawasaki.

Power Units

Up until a few years ago, a figure of 6,500 rpm was commonly the limit for regular production motorcycle engines. The Japanese motorcycle industry has pushed the rpm peak into the 9,000 range without loss of reliability. This they did by building unusually small-displacement and short-stroke units, and by keeping piston speeds and inertia loadings within practical limits despite the high crankshaft speeds involved. Only in Italy has this Japanese trend been followed to any degree. In the English motorcycle industry, which continues to produce the bulk of the world's supply of sporting motorcycles and machines in excess of 350 cubic centimeters, the Japanese trend has not been followed.

The question of whether additional power is best obtained by higher rpm or by increased piston displacement is rather

54

involved. The history of the American automotive industry has been simply a steady increase in piston displacement to achieve additional performance, despite the fact that many of these relatively short-stroke automotive engines could operate safely at appreciably higher rpm.

In summing up this aspect of motorcycle engine design, it is noteworthy that it may be more costly to achieve a specific power output and road performance on a very small engine operating at exceedingly high rpm than with a rather larger engine achieving the same power output at appreciably lower rpm. Home-market conditions and manufacturing costs in both Japan and Italy have enabled this small-displacement high-rpm engine trend to develop successfully but it would have been disastrous for motorcycle manufacturers in other countries, notably England and the United States, to have attempted to follow suit. In studying the performance and durability of these high-revving small-displacement units from Japan, no fault can be found. They have established a record of durability and reliability that compares favorably with many larger engines operating at much lower revs.

A few significant facts are now well established. The smaller units are generally quieter and require less starting effort. There is little difference in the matter of operating economy. Some of these small units, when driven very hard, do show up less favorably in the matter of gas mileage than larger units. To achieve reasonable performance with the very small engine units, it is essential to make full use of the gearbox. On larger engines, of course, vastly less gear shifting is required. For many riders this is an important consideration.

Certainly the greatest achievements in the line of improved performance in recent years have been in the two-stroke engine field, the two most notable developments being the rotary disc inlet valve and the wide adoption of automatic lubrication on Japanese two-strokes. Both, incidentally, are revivals of very old ideas. Automatic oiling on two-strokes was pioneered by the English manufacturers Scott and Velocette many years ago, as was a rotary disc inlet valve by the German DKW. Eliminating the need for mixing oil with gasoline has made the two-stroke engine much more acceptable. The refinement of throttle control to the oil pump has resulted in substantially reduced

Side-valve enthusiasts the world over will welcome revival, by Floyd Clymer, of the Indian 750 cc Scout. This 45 cubic-incher will be manufactured in West Germany and Italy for sale in the U.S.A.

The Yamaha Racer is a four-cylinder, water-cooled two-stroker. The two greatest developments in this field are the rotary disc inlet valve and the wide adoption of automatic lubrication system.

oil consumption, and the variation of oil supply to suit load conditions has proved beneficial to performance and durability.

On the question of future developments in motorcycle engine sizes, there can be little doubt that the very small units, particularly the 50-60 cc sizes, have had their day and there will be a steady trend to larger-displacement engines.

Looking to the future on engine layouts, it seems certain that low-cost utility models for the future will continue to have chiefly single cylinders, and there will not likely be any single-cylinder units developed in excess of 250 cc displacement.

In the twin-cylinder field, the range is presently from 100 to 1,200 cc. Most new models will likely be in the 500-750 cc range. In the popular 250 cc twin two-stroke class, 350 cc models are rapidly taking over and the most recent Suzuki model, a 500 cc twin, is likely the forerunner of other larger displacement two-stroke models.

Size for size, two-stroke engines now outstrip OHV and OHC four-stroke types for maximum power output and there appears to be no hope that the four-stroke motors can regain the absolute superiority enjoyed for so many years in the matter of maximum power output. It appears almost certain, however, that four-stroke

engines will continue to dominate the market in the 500 cc and larger sizes simply because of the relatively lower thermal efficiency of two-stroke engines, which results in a gas consumption some 30 to 50 per cent higher than the average four-stroke. The poor gas consumption characteristic of the two-stroke engine is most pronounced on high-performance types.

In the four-stroke engine field, the push rod-operated overhead-valve type still predominates in the larger sizes, although Honda now features the overhead camshaft almost exclusively. The side-valve unit has almost disappeared from the motorcycle scene. Presently, the only production side-valve engine unit is the 200 cc opposed-twin water-cooled Velocette manufactured in England. It is shortly to be joined by a revived Indian 750 cc Scout manufactured in Germany and Italy by Floyd Clymer. This development will be welcomed by side-valve enthusiasts the world over.

In the field of cylinder layouts there is not much new on the horizon except the three-cylinder 750 cc Triumph and BSA engine units that have been under development for some years. It seems likely that this layout will gradually replace the larger displacement vertical-twin models because of the much-improved crankshaft balance that will be achieved. The main advantage of a three-cylinder unit of this type over a four-cylinder, is the reduced width. The four-cylinder layout is a little wide for convenient transverse installation.

Objectionable vibration periods are common to most twin-cylinder layouts, excepting the 180° opposed, and the popular vertical-parallel twin is no exception, particularly in the larger sizes. The majority of the four-stroke twin models of this type have 360° crankshafts with alternate, evenly spaced firing intervals of 360°. Some Honda models have been produced with 180° crankshafts. Although this improves mechanical balance, the firing intervals are rather unevenly spaced at 180° and 540° and there is no indication of any general adoption of this crankshaft layout. The 180° crankshaft layout, however, is ideal for two-stroke twin models providing evenly, 180° spacing of firing intervals.

A recent Norton development to combat vibration problems is found in the new 750 cc Commando model in which rubber mounting of the engine and gearbox assembly in the frame is featured. This may well give the Norton a distinct lead over other large-displacement vertical twins that have objectionable vibration periods.

Unquestionably, it will be in the 500-750 cc range that the most interesting developments can be expected. More 500 twin two-strokes are in the cards. Various overhead-camshaft twins in the 750 cc range and 750 cc three-cylinder models are certain to be offered to cater to the demand for larger engines offering adequate performance under all conditions.

The two types of twin-cylinder layouts that have been in production since the early days of the motorcycle industry, but do not show too much promise of further adoption, are the "V" and opposed-cylinder layouts. The V-twin is one of the oldest types of motorcycle twin-cylinder designs and has been in steady production by Harley-Davidson for almost 60 years. This 45° twin layout features firing intervals of 405° and 315°. Although fitting rather conveniently into the conventional frame, inherent disadvantages of the V-twin are inferior carburetion and cooling characteristics.

The opposed twin, theoretically, is one of the best twin-cylinder layouts. A 180° crankshaft is used and the pistons travel outwards and inwards together with alternate firing intervals of 360°. Excellent mechanical balance, smoothness at all engine speeds and freedom from vibration are well-established characteristics of this layout. The German BMW is the best-known example of this type, currently being produced in 500 and 600 cc sizes.

Gearboxes

For many years the four-speed gearbox of constant-mesh type with foot-shift has been featured throughout the motorcycle industry. In recent years a few five-speed and six-speed units have been introduced. The latter are primarily an advantage over the two-stroke engines of high-performance type that deliver near-maximum torque throughout a rather narrow rpm band. For everyday use, on machines of adequate piston displacement and good torque characteristics, the four-speed gearbox can be considered adequate.

If five- or six-speed gearboxes were developed to provide an extra-low bottom gear for trail riding, this development would find more favor with many riders than the existing arrangement of simply

This is the 350 cc Honda four-cylinder four-stroke. The major motor developments have been the high-rpm capabilities of the small-displacements overhead-valve and overhead-camshaft Honda engines.

57

using the extra gears to provide closer spacing of ratios.

Although some separate-unit gearboxes are still being produced, notably in the Norton-Matchless range, some form of unit or semiunit construction of the engine and gearbox is now common throughout the motorcycle industry and almost certainly future designs will follow this trend.

Clutches

One of the weakest components throughout the motorcycle industry has been the clutch. With just a few exceptions, most clutches have very little reserve capacity and are subject either to slipping, under severe conditions, or failing to disengage fully, causing difficult gear changing because of drag.

Multiplate clutches on the gearbox mainshaft running at rather less than one half engine speed are common. On most types, clutch plates are not protected from primary-drive oil which minimizes the load capacity. Improvement on load capacity and durability in the clutch department will be best achieved with the crankshaft type operating at engine speed. This will give rather double the load capacity with similar .spring pressure to the existing countershaft type. A dry-type plate will ensure further improvement in load capacity. A diaphragm-type spring can be expected to replace the existing multicoil-spring arrangements when manufacturers finally get around to the overdue job of complete clutch redesign.

Power Drives

Roller chain continues to dominate. In recent years on primary drives there has been a trend from a single row to duplex and (on some of the more powerful machines) triplex chain. This trend probably will continue. A number of Japanese models feature gear-type primary drive that is highly satisfactory.

It is on the rear drive that most motorcycle manufacturers are very much behind the times. With just a few exceptions, an inadequately guarded and poorly lubricated chain is the standard rear drive throughout the motorcycle industry. The standard of reliability and durability is appalling. Adjustment, in many instances, is required as frequently as every 500 miles

The Honda 450 twin-cylinder four-stroke engine: the push rod-operated overhead-valve type predominates in larger sizes, although Honda uses overhead cams almost entirely.

and a life as short as 5,000 miles is not uncommon. Adequate enclosure, built-in oil supply and a means of automatic adjustment—something more satisfactory than moving the rear wheel in the frame—must certainly come soon.

What probably has deterred many manufacturers from the adoption of shaft drive is that existing motorcycle engine and gearbox layouts do not lend themselves to this installation and a complete redesign is required to satisfactorily incorporate it. Although in the sporting field the exposed rear-chain drive has been a convenience in the matter of sprocket changes for gearing alterations, the vast majority of motorcycle riders have no occasion to alter gearing and would be infinitely better served by an adequately enclosed, lubricated, and easily adjusted rear chain or an almost-maintenance-free shaft-drive layout. It is to be hoped that motorcycle manufacturers will soon give priority to rear-drive improvements.

Frames

A wide variety of frame designs are found in the motorcycle industry. Seamless steel tubing has been most generally used in motorcycle frame construction since the beginning of the industry. Brazed joints with forged steel or cast lugs have been gradually replaced with welding. On tube-type frames, the single front-down-tube type continues to enjoy wide use, together with the duplex-cradle-type frame. Although round-sectioned tubing is most generally used, there has been limited application of tapered- and oval-sectioned tubing, enabling better disposition of strength and weight-saving to be effected. Square tubing and rectangular-section frame members are recent developments in motorcycle frame construction and their use is not yet widespread.

The most significant trend in frame construction in recent years has been the "spine" type of frame, the "spine" or "backbone" generally being made of two pressings welded together. This main frame section runs from the steering head to the rear of the gearbox and from it the engine and gearbox unit are suspended. This frame construction offers cost savings where high-production volume is involved, together with some weight-saving and improved engine accessibility. There are some disadvantages to this layout, however. There is lack of crankcase protec-tion provided by the normal frame, and other provision has to be found for the mounting of such items as rear brake pedal and foot rests. This type of layout also fails to provide attachment points for such accessories as safety bars.

The swinging-arm type of hydraulic rear-frame suspension has now become universal throughout the motorcycle industry and there appears little need for any alterations in existing rear suspensions.

Front Forks

The well-known telescopic type of front forks with hydraulic control continues to be the most popular type throughout the motorcycle industry. The only other type in extensive use features lower links with hydraulic-suspension units somewhat similar to the rear-frame type. The latter type have the widest use in utility models made in Japan and are also found on certain English trials models. The lower-link-type forks offer some advantage in maintaining a fairly constant "trail" throughout the wheel movement and are possibly less sensitive to accident damage.

Wheels and Brakes

Except for a growing adoption of twin-cam front brakes, there is really nothing new in this field. A few disc brakes have been made for racing machines and used experimentally but are not standard equipment on any production models.

The last few years have witnessed further adoption of the full-width hub. Spoke-type wheels continue to be universal. A number of sporting models feature aluminium-alloy wheel rims. Although these offer some weight-saving they are certainly not up to steel rims for everyday use and are much more subject to damage under conditions of rough use. The trend to small wheel sizes has ended and it seems likely most new models will feature rims in a 17- to 18-inch range.

Weather Protection

Despite the fact that many motorcyclists who use their machine for everyday transporation would welcome improved weather protection, it appears that design trends in the motorcycle industry are going to continue to be set by sporting considerations. There is no indication of any trend toward extensive engine enclosure or windshield-fairing equipment being adopted as standard wear. Riders who want weather protection will likely have to continue to make their own installation.

Racing Developments

The trend of racing developments has always been of great interest to motorcycle enthusiasts everywhere. Unfortunately, in recent years, of necessity, racing machines have become highly specialized projectiles with power units bearing little relationship to production motors. Although racing has, and will continue no doubt to make some contributions in the research field to overall motorcycle improvement, there is little doubt that racing has outlived its usefulness in the development of motorcycles for everyday use.

The type of motorcycle that now must be developed to succeed in international events bears practically no relationship to the everyday motorcycle. For this reason, many manufacturers who did support motorcycle racing in the past have given up this activity. Provided manufacturers do apply themselves with suitable dedication to the general improvement of motorcycle design with adequate appreciation of the importance of improved standards of durability, greater progress can almost certainly be achieved at less cost by avoiding participation in the building of specialized racing machines.

To be successful in international racing events for the immediate future requires engine rpm capabilities in the 15,000 range and power outputs in excess of 3 hp per cubic inch of piston displacement. Multicylinder engines with individual piston displacements as small as 40 cc are now required.

For all-out maximum power, size for size, the water-cooled multicylinder two-stroke appears to be the motor to beat. The racing two-stroke motor has a much narrower usable power band than racing four-stroke engines, and, despite higher maximum power output potential, may well continue to prove inferior to the four-stroke in many types of competition events.

Although many excellent features found in production motorcycles today owe their inception or development to racing activity, at the same time many design trends that are fundamentally wrong for average use have been promoted.

Future Prospects

Nothing in the line of substantially different power units is in sight. We are not likely to see turbine engines on motorcycles. Almost certainly the piston engine will continue supreme for many years to come. A trend to rather larger-displacement engines is a certainty. Air-cooling,

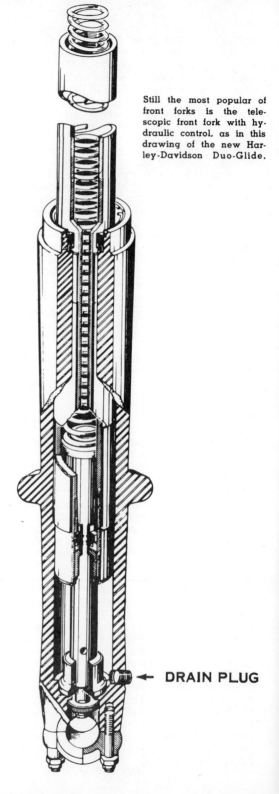

Still the most popular of front forks is the telescopic front fork with hydraulic control, as in this drawing of the new Harley-Davidson Duo-Glide.

← **DRAIN PLUG**

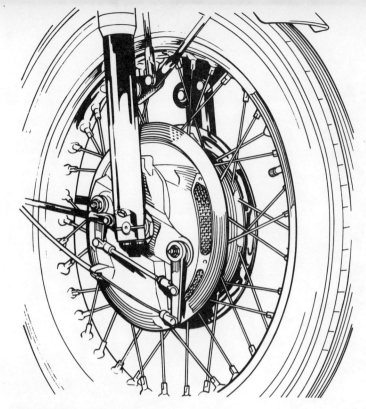

Twin-leading shoe front brakes are now common on motorcycles. In the drawing, note the rod linking the two brake arms on this Triumph 650 cc model.

because of its simplicity, will continue on all but a limited number of special racing machines. On these, water-cooling may be necessary to provide sustained power output.

To reduce the high mortality rate on existing air-cooled motorcycle engines because of temperatures climbing beyond safe limits, unknown to the operator, a cylinder-head temperature gauge is long overdue as standard equipment on some high-performance models. This is a development that can be anticipated.

Another engine safeguard that would be particularly useful to avoid engine destruction from over-revving, particularly in competition riding when a gear change may be missed at full throttle, would be an electrically operated ignition cutout that could be set to operate at any desired rpm. This is something to be thought of for the future.

One of the main problems with the motorcycle industry continues to be the wide variety of models. As a result, parts supply and servicing is complicated. It is to be hoped that there will be some reduction in the number of models produced, enabling more-concentrated improvements together with fewer parts supply and servicing problems. All manufacturers could do well to give a little more thought to improved durability and reduction in maintenance requirements. It is probably in this field that the motorcycle industry has most of all failed to keep pace with automobile standards.

There is, unfortunately, among many manufacturers today, an apathy in the matter of standards of durability and reliability. This situation is well illustrated by a number of manufacturers failing to use chrome-plated piston rings as standard equipment, although it is well established that these do extend both piston-ring and cylinder-bore life to as much as three times that of regular rings. Air filtration and oil filtration on many machines continues to be most inadequate for worldwide service conditions, resulting in premature wear.

Conclusions

A general study of motorcycle design is a fascinating experience. The motorcycle industry is probably without equal in the mechanical field for the variety of makes, models, and designs produced. The amount of development work that has been undertaken by the industry as a whole, in relation to total motorcycle production, is remarkable. Motorcycle enthusiasts can anticipate future developments in the motorcycle industry of great interest in the utility, sporting, and all-out racing fields. •

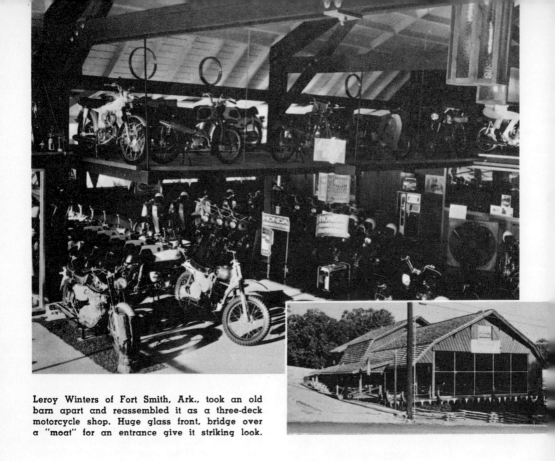

Leroy Winters of Fort Smith, Ark., took an old barn apart and reassembled it as a three-deck motorcycle shop. Huge glass front, bridge over a "moat" for an entrance give it striking look.

How to Choose a
Motorcycle Dealer

By Jack B. Mercer

"Honest John" Mercer has been a road man for three motorcycle importers and one parts distributor over the past two decades.

THE AUTHOR'S experience goes back to The Dark Ages of American motorcycling, those prewar days when the choice was simple: You rode an Indian, or you rode a Harley-Davidson, and seldom would you be found in the enemy camp. Like rival religions, we each had our temple. In some towns the two cycle shops might face each other, and it was like a scene from the movie High Noon to watch the glowering bad looks exchanged across the No-Man's

Land of Main St. Such prejudice would be impossible today because the game is so much bigger, and so many wonderful, crazy makes are available. In fact, there are so many brands trying to gain a foothold in the U. S. market that a few tips on choosing a dealer may help newcomers to the sport.

While it's obvious that the name of the game is Service, there are other factors to consider in choosing one's motorcycle dealer. Let's start with some basic terms so that we can understand one another.

Motorcycle: "Bike" to some, "cycle" to others, and "sickle" to the boys out in the country; but it all means the same thing—a two-wheeled motorized bit of tranportation that is many things to almost two million Americans. Once hooked on motorcycling, a guy stays with it for the rest of his life. If we could invite General Eisenhower or Charles Lindbergh to this party they would surely reminisce about their Harley days. That's how strong the bug can bite. Whether you ride on the highways, engage in scrambling, knock yourself out in mud runs, or even fly with the gods on flat track or road circuit, you are part of the two-wheeled sport and your life will always be richer for it.

Service: "One hour on the road, two hours in the shop," my Dad use to say when he found me working on my ancient Indian Scout. He was right, because whether the bike was running well or not, I inspected it regularly—this was part of the fun of ownership. One thing about a motorcycle: It may look like the simplest kind of internal-combustion engine, but it can be much more complex than a V-8. Simple car jobs, like fixing a flat or changing a wheel, can be both time-consuming or next-to-impossible with a motorcycle. Each machine comes equipped with a bundle of tools that don't quite do all the jobs, and The Riders Manual is not always written to the level of the naive new owner. So, lacking sufficient tools and info, we must occasionally go for help to the guy euphemistically termed "Your Friendly Dealer" in the advertisements. Whether this guy treats you as friend or foe depends on how well you utilize the following hints and tips.

The Dealers: Most dealers started as enthusiasts. Some were so sure they could beat the lousy service of the old dealer that they trapped themselves into what can often be a tough way of making a living. The good dealers are always service minded. Some are so shy about selling that they hide from prospective customers. Obviously, the perfect dealer is the enthusiast who likes to sell and insists on proper service. This typifies the successful dealer, the guy who will be around for years and years —a man you can depend upon to back the product he sold to you, whether he might drop that particular franchise at a later time, or not. The whole store should reflect enthusiasm, interest, sales and service. It should be a nice, warm place to want to visit. After all, we are concerned with a sport, not just transportation. But, more on The Dealer, later.

The Brands

The kind of service you can expect will depend a great deal on which of the many brands you buy. Almost any motorcycle will have the expected performance characteristics, but not all the brands can match performance with service. So, here are some general observations on service, leaving the sales pitch to the manufacturers.

Harley-Davidson: One of the oldest and best-serviced of the lot. Its Service School

Hank Slegers of Whippany, N. J., built this paneled showroom for his Honda, Triumphs, BSAs and BMWs. A large shop is behind counter, right.

John Esler of Grand Rapids, Mich., uses one-third of this modern new building for displaying Triumphs, BMWs, two-thirds for service facilities.

Norm Reeves of Los Angeles houses an enormous stock of Hondas inside and outside his vast store in Paramount, a suburb of L.A. A large side yard, not visible, handles overflow.

is still the finest; in fact, many of the dealers in imported bikes got their start as mechanics at the Harley school. Like Volkswagen agencies, Harley-Davidson dealers try to avoid working on anything but their own brand. Few Harley dealers carry other bikes. When they do, however, they generally give the same faithful service. While riders of imported machinery like to kid the owners of the big Harley Twins, they can only envy the consistently good Milwaukee service record.

British: The big British brands are now Triumph, BSA and Norton, in that order. Many once-popular postwar names like Ariel, Velocette and Vincent are no more, and The Big Three are working hard to stay in the U. S. All three makes go like

blue-blazes and show up in the winning circle enough times to be popular with the hot-rodders who like dazzling performance. Because many of these brand dealers carry other makes, their shops are interesting to visit. Some of the larger guys might have over 100 different motorcycles to look at. How they service half-a-dozen makes is a mystery, but many succeed. It is not unusual to find a foreign-machine customer with several bikes, starting with a small, rugged woods toy and ending with an accessory-loaded road bike. The Big Three have become so popular that independent accessory manufacturers have found a market for special parts, most of these being attempts to increase power output. Special cams, sprockets, and exhaust systems add to the fun and color of owning one of these British Bombs.

Japanese: Honda is still No. 1 by far, with Yamaha pushing close in certain areas. Suzuki, Kawasaki, Bridgestone and a host of smaller specialty bikes, like Hodaka, must also be mentioned. Few dealers in Japanese machinery are exclusive anymore, and most have added one of the bigger British lines to catch the small-bike owner who wants to trade up. While service backing has been good for the popular Japanese makes, there has been a terrific dealer turnover and the business mortality rate has been high in recent years. This is especially true of the car types who got into the motorcycle market to make a fast buck, and left when the going got tough. The moral is obvious: Favor the *real* motorcycle man who is going to stay in the trade.

German: Right after World War II there were almost as many German makes as British, but this has changed, radically, and only BMW remains with much strength. The big, quiet BMW is growing, but will almost always be found in combination with a British make, or even Harley-Davidson. Dependability and good service is a mark of this brand. Lately, we are seeing a slight resurgence of a few German two-cycle engine makes, but this is small and puts them in the same special category as other small-production makes.

Italian: Ducati is the big name at this writing and it will generally be found at the Norton shop. Benelli, Moto-Guzzi, Gilera and certain other hard-to-pronounce Italian brands are around, many sold by chain-store catalog companies. This is done because the regular sales channels are not open for as many brands as would like to get a handle on the U.S. market.

Specials: Here we lump all of the many small-production makes, regardless of country of origin, that are found in motorcycle shops. These include scrambling bikes like Greeves, CZ, Husqvarna, and a host of Spanish makes led by Bultaco, Montessa and Ossa. In general, service on these makes will reflect the enthusiasm of the dealer who sells them. If the dealer is not part of the sport, he will probably not do much more than take your money for the bike. After that, you must join The Orphans.

The Orphans: These are what is left— the brands listed in Sears-Roebuck's, Ward's and Siegel's mail-order catalogs, plus those brands sold in chain-saw outlets, tire company stores, and so on. Service on any of these ranges from poor to nonexistent. Parts are also hard to obtain. Expect long waits for spares. Also, be prepared for. disinterested treatment by people who are not really in the motorcycle business. The catalog houses only want to get the young cyclist in the habit of buying from them. They count on the young man who got his small bike on a "No Money Down and a Coupla Bucks a Month" to come back after he is married to buy his house furnishings and kids' clothes the same way. Not many of these customers graduate to the ranks of motorcycling regulars, and it would be hard to find a more unhappy group of cyclists in America. Obviously, if you want a motorcycle, go to a motorcycle shop.

Conclusions

Let's return now to The Dealer we left at the beginning. Assuming that the reader of this chapter is a newcomer to motorcycling and perhaps not yet an owner, we'll recap by the numbers.

1. A motorcycle is a very special vehicle, despite its simple appearance, and requires proper care from specially trained men.

2. The motorcycle dealer is the only specialist who can perform the necessary services. Your job is to find the best-qualified dealer to take care of you and your bike. Obviously, if the man chosen also sells you a mount, he will have a good reason for taking better care of your needs. A word of warning: Don't argue too much on price. After all, the motorcycle business is very seasonal in most parts of the country and requires full profit on goods and services. Further, the cycle store is practically a year-round club for many of its customers, a place where riders visit even during the frozen months. If the dealer is a good guy and an enthusiast, and he has made a buck on you, he won't mind swapping stories, letting you read his latest magazines, and even sharing his coffee at no fee.

3. Check around with other riders and get their stories on bikes and dealers. Don't accept these stories as gospel, though, but go visit the cycle shops on your own and ask the dealer straight, honest questions. If he is the right guy, you will get the message. Finally, if you don't know motorcycles, know your motorcycle dealer. It is just as important to find the right dealer as it is to locate the right motorcycle. Avoid falling for "The Big Bargain" and getting stuck with an Orphan because this could be a very expensive mistake.

Lots of luck, and many miles of happy riding! •

Motorcycle Tours in Europe

MOTORCYCLES and touring are a natural combination—you see more, at less expense, than any other way. Americans have been criss-crossing the United States and Europe on bikes for decades, alone or in small groups. What's new is the growth of organized tours on a continuing basis.

Now you can simply pay a remarkably low flat price, get a passport, visas, smallpox vaccination, and international driver's license and be off. A common feature of the group tour is purchase of a new motorcycle as part of the arrangement. Or you can go along with a motorcycle tour, but ride all the way in a bus. And one tour's purpose is just to watch the Isle of Man championship races; no riding by tour members is involved. So there are plenty of options.

The three tours described here have each had at least one successful season under their belts and promise to keep going indefinitely. Thus, even though it's too late to get in on the 1968 tours described, there will be annual tours in later years similar to these.

Edison Dye's Rally in Europe

The 1968 rally will be Edison Dye's fifth annual group trip to Europe, which

These are minimum prices, of course. Though they include passenger air fares, purchase of motorcycle and air freight to New York, and for its hotels and many meals, they do not cover everything. Several hundred dollars more should be allowed for vehicle insurance, tolls, gasoline (high in Europe), tips for tour guides, and the inevitable souvenirs. KLM Royal Dutch Airlines, the international carrier, has a 24-month financing plan available for its part of the cost.

Here's what the itinerary for the 1968 Edison Dye Rally in Europe looks like:

May 23—Fly from New York.
May 24—Arrive in Amsterdam. BMW riders fly to Munich. Triumph riders fly to London, pick up bikes, fly back across the Channel, and ride some 450 miles to Munich in two days.
May 25—BMW riders sight-see in Munich and pick up bikes at factory.
May 26—Full group rides through Oberammergau, Garmisch-Partenkirchen, and Innsbruck to Worgel.
May 27—Ride through Berchtesgaden and Salzburg to St. Wolfgang.
May 28—Sight-see in St. Wolfgang and on the Wolfgang-See (lake).
May 29—Ride through Bad Ischl, Bad Ausee, Liezen and Hieflau coming to

makes him the granddaddy of this activity. In 1966 he operated a Scandinavian Safari, but the standard tour in 1968 is centered on Munich. It makes an oval-shaped circuit through southern West Germany, Austria, northern Italy and Switzerland.

How much it costs depends on where you start from, and which of five motorcycles you order to ride. If you leave from New York or Montreal and order a BMW R-50, for example, it costs $1,550. If you leave from Los Angeles and order a BMW R-69S it costs $2,185. Other prices fall between these extremes. You can also have a BMW R-60, Triumph TR-6, or Triumph Bonneville. The fare from Chicago is $114 more than from New York or Montreal; the fare from Los Angeles is $304 more.

You can take your girl friend or wife along for $679 extra from New York or Montreal, $752 extra from Chicago, and $939 extra from Los Angeles.

Group of riders take time out from race for coffee break while on the road to Brussels, Belgium.

Right, tour members line up behind their Volkswagen Microbus in Riva, Italy—19 bikes in all.

It's easy to understand the popularity of the Edison Singles Swingers Tour. She's a guide.

Members of Eur-Cycle Tour pose in Dutch costumes. Director Ted von der Kolk holds accordion, right.

Klosterneuburg just outside Vienna, Austria.

May 30—Sight-see in Vienna.

May 31—Ride through Wiener Neustadt, Neunkirchen, Mürzzuschlag, Bruck and Frohnleiten to Weiz.

June 1—Ride through Wolfsberg, St. Andrae, Klagenfurt, Villach, Spittal and Lienz to Cortina de Ampezzo, Italy.

June 2—Ride through Balzano and Trento to Riva.

June 3—Sight-see in Riva.

June 4—Ride to Brescia, Bergamo, Milan and Turin to Aosta.

June 5—Ride through Grand St. Bernard Pass, Chamonix and St. Vergais to Geneva, Switzerland.

June 6—Ride through Bern to Zurich.

June 7—Ride through Meersburg to Fussen, West Germany.

June 8—Ride to Starnberg, just outside Munich. Spend afternoon sight-seeing in Munich.

June 9—Fly to London, then to Isle of Man.

June 10—Watch sidecar and 250 cc motorcycle races on Isle of Man.

June 11—Sight-see on Isle of Man, watch Grand National Scrambles Championship in evening.

June 12—Watch 125 cc and 350 cc motorcycle races on Isle of Man.

June 13—Fly back to New York.

During the tour's three weeks, the Triumph riders cover roughly 2,000 miles in 16 days and the BMW riders cover about 1,500 in 14 days. In bad weather passengers can ride in the Volkswagen Microbus with the baggage and the BMW factory mechanic. But the riders go regardless, since the hotels have been reserved long in advance for particular nights. Nonetheless, tour members have ranged in age from 20 to 75. Good health and adequate riding experience are the only prerequisites.

Single Swingers Tour

Edison Dye will run a second three-week tour for the first time in 1968. It's intended for the young single man in his 20s who wants to see Europe and enjoy himself socially at the same time. A limit of 20 has been set on the number. The gimmick is that each tour member, besides buying his own BMW, will have a European college student (female) ride with him as a guide throughout the trip. Torsten Hallman and Joel Robert, world moto-cross champions, will play host at the start in Brussels, Belgium. Then tour members ride through Nancy (France),

Basel, Geneva, Grenoble, Marseilles, St. Tropez, Isle of Levant, Monte Carlo, the Italian Riviera, Milan, Riva, St. Wolfgang and Munich. Bikes and tour members will be flown back to New York from Munich; the girls will return to Belgium by bus. No prices were available for this Single Swingers Tour. Write to MoTours Travel, Box 3571, San Diego, Calif., 92103 for complete information and application blank on Edison Tours.

Ted van der Kolk Eur-Cycle Tours

The 1968 tour of Europe will be Ted van der Kolk's second annual event. The route begins and ends in Amsterdam, heading almost due south as far as Rome and jogging over into France for a return through Paris. There are two options on route, however. You can stay on the continent the whole time or break off from the main group for a few days at the Isle of Man races near the end.

As with the other tour, price for Eur-Cycle Tours depends on the motorcycle you buy. All price quotes include round trip air fare from New York only, but the company makes all arrangements to fly you from Los Angeles or Chicago, and the additional air fare is quoted on request. Motorcycles are shipped to the seaport nearest your home at the end of the tour.

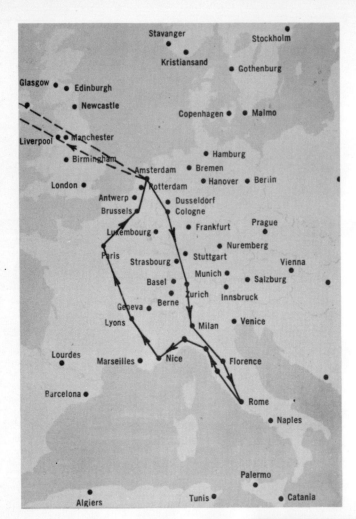

The map shows cities across Europe including Stavanger, Stockholm, Kristiansand, Gothenburg, Glasgow, Edinburgh, Newcastle, Copenhagen, Malmo, Liverpool, Manchester, Birmingham, Hamburg, Bremen, Amsterdam, Hanover, Berlin, London, Rotterdam, Antwerp, Dusseldorf, Brussels, Cologne, Prague, Luxembourg, Frankfurt, Nuremberg, Paris, Strasbourg, Stuttgart, Vienna, Munich, Salzburg, Basel, Zurich, Innsbruck, Geneva, Berne, Lyons, Milan, Venice, Lourdes, Marseilles, Nice, Florence, Barcelona, Rome, Naples, Palermo, Algiers, Tunis, Catania.

At left, map shows itinerary of Eur-Cycle tour. The route begins and ends in Amsterdam, south to Rome.

BMW sidecar (below), piloted by S. Schauzee with H. Schneider as passenger, came home first in race.

A group of Hank Slegers' tour members relax in front of their hotel in Douglas, on Isle of Man.

Sidecar sweeps around S curve at Braddan Bridge, Isle of Man. Sidecar acrobatics get spectacular on sharp turns.

Motorcycles available are the Matchless G-80 and G-15; AJS 18 and 33; the Norton 650 SS, Atlas, P-11 and Commando; Triumph (prices on request); and BMW R-50, R-60 and R-69S. The lowest price for a standard tour is $1,535 with a Matchless G-80 or AJS 18; the highest is $2,125 for a BMW R-69S. For switching to the Isle of Man junket at the end there is an additional charge of $55.

An extra passenger can come along and ride in a "de luxe motorcoach" with the baggage for $739. You can also buy a sidecar for your machine—prices on request. You can pay all but $200 for the tour's cost, including the cost of the motorcycle, over three to 24 months.

Here's the Eur-Cycle Tour itinerary:

May 22—Fly from New York on KLM Royal Dutch Airlines.

May 23—Arrive in Amsterdam, pick up motorcycles, and sight-see in Amsterdam.

May 24—Ride through Utrecht and Arnhem to Cologne, Germany.

May 25—Ride through Bonn and Koblenz to Heidelberg.

May 26—Ride through the Black Forest and Zurich to Luzern, Switzerland.

May 27—Sight-see in Luzern, then ride over St. Gotthard Pass to Bellinzona.

May 28—Ride through Lugano and Como to Milan. Sight-see in Milan.

May 29—Ride to Florence.

May 30—Sight-see in Florence, then ride on to Rome.

May 31—Sight-see in Rome for two days.

June 2—Ride through Civitavecchia, Tarquinia, Grosseto, Pisa, and Viareggio to La Spezia.

June 3—Ride through Rapallo, Genoa, San Remo, Ventimiglia, Menton and Monte Carlo to Nice, France.

June 4—Sight-see in Nice. (Isle of Man tour members split off and take train to Paris. They spend time in Paris, London and the Isle of Man (for the races) before going back to Amsterdam for their return flight to New York.)

June 5—Ride through Grasse, Digne, Sisteron, and Grenoble to Lyon.

June 6—Ride through Mâcon, Chalon-sur-Saône, Avallon, Auxerre and Fountainebleu to Paris.

June 7—Sight-see in Paris for two days.

June 9—Ride through Amiens, Cambrai and Mons to Brussels, Belgium.

June 10—Sight-see in Brussels, then ride through Antwerp to Amsterdam.

June 11—Sight-see in Amsterdam.

June 12—Fly to New York.

During the three weeks, the Isle of Man tourists cover about 1,600 miles in 12 days of riding; the standard tour covers roughly 2,500 miles in 18 days. As with the other tours, schedules must be met or you're on your own. The longest one-day run is about 300 miles, the shortest is only 63 miles.

Hank Slegers Isle of Man Tour

The 1968 tour is Hank Slegers' second to the Isle of Man. There are no motorcycles to buy or ride; it's strictly a spectator affair. The price for each of the 35 tourists, therefore, is only $235. This covers air fare to and from New York. Bring another $100 for hotels and meals during the two weeks.

Besides watching the races, during the tour, there will be a visit to the Triumph factory and another one at the BSA factory. During the visit, the group will be guests at lunch and supper.

A bus tour, while in Birmingham, will include a visit to Stratford-on-Avon and

Above, riders line up for the 500 cc race. No. 1 is a Matchless, No. 4 a Honda 4, No. 9 is an MV Agusta.

A 500 cc machine going 140 mph streaks down Bray Hill on a Douglas street half-mile from start.

dinner at the famous White Swan Inn. Those interested can attend a play given by the Shakespearean repertory theatre group in Stratford.

Write for details and application to Hank Slegers Co., Inc., 19 Ridgedale Ave., Whippany, New Jersey, 07981.

Conclusions

Tours are an ideal way to see a lot in a short time, combine an enthusiasm for travel with an enthusiasm for motorcycling, and do it inexpensively. These three tours indicate the variety available so far. There are bound to be more as time goes on. Here are a few tips to remember.

• Group sizes are limited, so apply early —six months ahead is barely enough.

• Be sure you can, and will want to, go through with your commitment once it's made. The closer you get to tour time the more money it will cost to pull out. Even if you can salvage some of the fare you may wind up with a motorcycle.

• Hotel accommodations are normally two to a room. If this bothers you, some single accommodations can probably be arranged for an additional charge. Eur-Cycle Tours offers this option for $50 more, for example.

• Tour members ride in small groups to reduce driving hazards, meet all together at whatever hotel has been designated for the night. There's no attempt to keep everyone together at all times. On leisure days you're on your own.

• Keeping to a schedule can be hard work, especially if the weather is windy, rainy or cold. Be prepared, mentally and physically, to do more riding than you're normally used to. If you drop out of the tour, you must pay your own way home.

• You can get a good idea how much riding and sight-seeing you will be doing by getting hold of a good atlas, or set of road maps, and tracing the itineraries given here. Esso, and other oil companies are a good source for road maps, so are the tourist bureaus of the countries to be visited.

• Don't try to figure your expenses too closely. Imagine what it would take to make a three-week trip in this country— gasoline, tolls, extra meals, tips, local sight-seeing and souvenirs. Play it safe; an extra $100 in traveler's checks is good insurance.

• Don't worry about breakdowns, the riding tours have mechanics. Do pick a machine you know you can handle—you'll be covering ground fast, right from the start.

• Finally, it's much more fun, and safer, going in a group with professional backup than wandering around by yourself. Unless, perhaps, you have unlimited time and money.

Here's the only mass start of the TT races. No. 1 is H. G. Anscheidt, world champion in 50 cc class.

Getting
Started
in Competition

By Bob Hicks

Bob Hicks, editor of Cycle Sport, is a long-time competitor in New England motorcycle events.

YOU'VE RIDDEN your street machine for a while now and begun to hear about local competition on the weekends. There's a grab bag full of events: field meets, road runs, modified reliability runs, trials, enduros, and scrambles. All are promoted by clubs in your area affiliated with the American Motorcycle Association (A.M.A.). You can find out about the events and the clubs from your nearest motorcycle dealer.

A field meet is one of the best ways to get started. You can use your street bike, the games are easy to play, and your fellow competitors are often as new at them as you are. Girl friends, wives, and youngsters usually join in; it's a real family-type affair.

You might ride your bike over a teeter-totter, weave back and forth through a row of slalom stakes, or creep down a field as *slowly* as possible without putting a foot down for balance. Or you might ride under a hot dog dangling from a string and try to take a bite out of it, or drive your girl quickly down the field as she balances an egg in a spoon clenched between her teeth. The variety of games is endless. You have a different kind of fun with your bike and may even be skillful enough—or lucky enough—to win a trophy.

A road run takes the same riding skills and machine as you've been using every day. But you will have to develop a specialized navigating ability; a few simple accessories will help too.

Before you start you're handed a route sheet that tells you the distances between turning points and the direction to go at each of them. The sheet also sets an

In this Field Meet the sponsoring club built a huge seesaw. Contestants rode up one side, gently tipped board to other side and rode down. Another game, at right, required passenger to pin bloomers on a line without taking feet off the bike, while rider waited, ready to dash back to finish line.

A modified reliability run usually goes over dirt roads and forest trails. This particular contest, at left, was run in New England.

average speed—usually 24 mph because there are exactly two miles to cover every five minutes, which is easy to figure.

You watch the odometer (one that registers tenths of a mile is best) to tell when to turn, watch the speedometer to stay on schedule generally, and look at an accurate watch regularly to hit check points right on time. You lose a point for each minute you arrive at a check point too early or too late. The competitor who loses the fewest points in each class—novice, amateur, expert—wins. Secret checks that time each rider to the second are used to break ties.

Some riders make route boards to hold their clocks or watches and their route sheets. But you can manage almost as well by using a wrist watch with sweep second hand and fastening the route sheet to your forearm, outside all clothing, with two heavy rubber bands.

A modified reliability run follows the same basic rules as a road run, except that it's over a tougher route. Much of it is off paved highways and on dirt roads or footpaths. You can usually make it with a road bike, though a heavy machine with low ground clearance can be a handicap. It takes more bike-handling and navigating skill than a road run, which makes it more fun. A so-called "road scrambler" would be well-suited to most modified reliability runs.

Trials consist of a series of short, very rough, sections in unpaved and unimproved country. You must guide your motorcycle between the tapes or lines that mark each section without stopping or putting your foot down—or falling off, of course. The terrain is usually very demanding and includes steep grades, tight turns around trees and rocks, and occasionally stream crossings. Some clubs lay out two trials courses, one for street bikes and one for trials bikes.

The speeds are low in trials riding; emphasis is on control of throttle, clutch, and your own body movements to maintain balance. Your street machine will do for courses laid out especially for them. But for the real trials courses you'll need a bike designed for the job. Usually it's relatively light, has a high ground clearance, low compression ratio, and good low-speed torque. You'll want one if the game really grabs you. A scrambles bike, incidentally, makes a poor trials bike; an enduro machine is sort of in between.

An enduro is a long-distance ride over old roads, trails, footpaths, brook crossings, power-line hills, sand, rocks. You name it, the enduro has it. As in the road run you

Whidden photos

Trials contestants take it slowly over steep, above, and often muddy and rocky sections, below. They must stay between lines and keep feet off the ground. It takes skillful control and concentration.

Enduros are the toughest events for bikes and riders. Water crossings are standard, so is mud. But these are toughest spots; most of the 100 miles, or so, are clear forest trails and dirt roads. Light bike and clothing are an asset—but skill and experience are the best accessories, after all.

Whidden photos

77

have to maintain a schedule, again usually 24 mph. But in an enduro this can seem impossible as you struggle through a long stretch of bog walking your bike. Often the sponsoring club makes path-finding much easier by posting directional arrows in the toughest sections.

You could try your road bike on a tame enduro, but you might regret it. Without a skid plate you could crack the crankcase, without knobby tires you could end up walking the bike up steep hills and through slippery terrain. Besides huge ground clearance, a skid plate, and knobby tires you need short fenders with plenty of clearance between them and the tires, a waterproofed ignition and carburetor, up-swept exhaust pipes, and a wide-ratio gearbox with a very low first gear.

Enduros run from 60 to 200 miles in a day. There are even two-day events, but they take very careful preparation and considerable experience. An enduro can be exhausting, but it's more of a battle between you and raw nature than a battle between competitors, which makes it as much fun for a beginner as for an old timer. Sometimes just finishing the course can be a proud achievement. Better go watch a few, then do some cow-trailing before entering one. Once you've gotten some

Scrambling is the queen of local competition. The courses vary from open meadow, above, to tree-lined sand banks, left. Second rider, left, on #5 is the author, Bob Hicks.

Eugénie photos

trail riding under your belt—in mud and ruts, over rocks, through brooks, on wet leaves, and the like—you'll be ready.

Scrambles are the single most popular motorcycle sporting event in the United States these days. It's real motorcycle racing for the average guy and it takes place in hundreds of places every Sunday, most of the year, on rough or smooth, tricky, twisty courses. Sheer speed is secondary to good bike handling. No cash is paid out—it's all for trophies and glory.

Probably you'd better go to some scrambles first to watch, and to see what sort of bike you'll need. Many areas have novice classes for beginners, who can remove the lights from their "street scramblers" and get into action. But if you get the bug you'll soon be shopping for a *real* scrambler. This machine is built to go fast over the ground, has different handling characteristics from the street bike. The front and rear suspensions boast far better, longer travel and damping—to keep the wheels on the ground regardless of terrain.

The scrambles bike will have a much racier engine, generally a single-cylinder two-stroke in the 250 cc or smaller classes, often a vertical-twin 650 cc machine in the big-bike groups. Riders are separated by the displacement of their bikes to make it fair. Often they're further divided into novice, amateur, and expert classes depending on how many events they're scored in. Since you're new to scrambling you'll start as a novice or amateur.

Here, too, some practice by yourself is a good idea, though it may be harder to manage for scrambling. Tracks are built on private property and you need permission to use them when they're not engaged for an event. But it's worth a try.

Whatever you think you'll like, go look it over and get into the act. You'll find a whole new world of motorcycling. And what if you aren't all that great at the game to start? You'll become one of the experts if you stick with it and get the right bike for the job. Whatever happens you'll enjoy yourself trying. •

Testing compression takes two people, one to hold gauge in the spark plug hole and the other to push down on the kickstarter pedal. That's mechanic Jack Creelman at left with boss Hank Slegers.

How to Test a Used Motorcycle

"**O**NE OF THE MOST miserable things in the world to buy is a used motorcycle," says Jack Creelman. A mechanic for the past 11 years, Jack should know. His boss, Hank Slegers, has been buying, selling, and fixing bikes for 14 years.

These two pros have put their experiences at Hank Slegers Co., Inc., in Whippany, N.J., together and come up with a wealth of tips that could save you money and grief. As franchised agents for BMW, BSA, Bultaco, Honda and Triumph their experience ranges over more ground than most dealers can match. And since their shop is open to any rider, they've had their hands on many other makes as well.

Actually you don't have to buy a second-hand bike to make use of these tips. Applied to your present machine, they will help you get greater pleasure and safer rides from it. Or they'll help you get a good price should you decide to sell or trade in.

General Appearance

You can test for many things on a motorcycle, but short of taking it all apart you can't find out all you'd like to know. For that reason the single most revealing aspect of a second-hand bike is its appearance. Basically, what you want to find out is what kind of a rider the previous owner was. A machine that looks scruffy outside—with broken and missing parts—has probably been abused consistently. That means the brakes, wiring, clutch, engine, gearbox, and even the frame may be in poor shape too.

One broken or missing part doesn't necessarily spell trouble, however. Anyone can have a minor accident. What you're looking for are signs of general neglect, leading you to suspect that the oil hasn't been changed much, the battery inspected periodically, the chain lubricated and adjusted, control cables renewed, wiring repaired, and so on.

For your own safety you should accept the fact that some machines aren't worth buying at *any* price. Let someone else ride with bald tires, a broken front brake cable, a missing chain guard or a bent frame. But unless you're willing to put the machine back in close-to-original shape, don't risk *your* life on it. Far better to buy a smaller bike in good condition than a big wreck.

Missing Parts

While you're checking over the bike's general appearance you can be looking for missing parts that will cost you money if you buy it. Starting at the front, here are parts most likely to be absent: front fender, front brake cable, rubber gaiters (boots) on front fork, headlight, speedometer cable, speedometer, front brake lever, gas cap, knee pads on gas tank, air cleaner on carburetor, kickstarter rubber, shift lever rubber, chain guard, muffler(s), stoplight switch, tail light and rear fender.

A brake cable, gaiters, gas cap, or control lever rubbers are more annoying than expensive to replace. But it costs $10 to 35 for a front fender, $10 to 40 for a headlight, $5 to 8 for a speedometer cable, $15 to 50 for a speedometer, $3 for a brake lever, $4 for a pair of rubber knee pads, $6 to 10 for an air cleaner, $10 to 15 for a chain guard, $10 for a small-bike muffler and $25 to 30 for a big bike, $3 to 5 for a stoplight switch, $5 to 10 for a tail light, and $15 to 45 for a rear fender. You can start your appraisal by totaling up the cost of any missing parts.

Tires and Wheels

Good tires are more important—and more expensive—on a motorcycle than a car. Check the tread depth with a tread-depth gauge if you can; they're sold for under a dollar by auto supply stores. A thin ruler will do almost as well. Unless there is at least $1/8$ inch of tread left you will need a new tire. A set of tires normally lasts between 10,000 and 15,000 miles, with the rear tires on big bikes usually wearing out first. The front tire, however, often cups (develops hollows) rather than wearing down evenly, so measure the *shallowest* part of the tread. Spaces between treads allow the tire to squeeze water off the road under the tire, thereby giving it a grip in the rain. So don't outwit yourself by measuring the deepest part of the tread.

You can save money on replacing a tire by removing the wheel or wheels and putting them back yourself. If you take just the wheels into a dealer you can have new rubber mounted for $13-15 on the front wheel of a medium-sized bike and for $17-

Peeling chrome on chain case was caused by battery above it "boiling over" from being over-filled or over-charged. Replacing ugly case will be expensive.

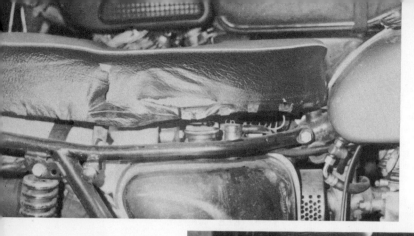

Torn saddle cover indicates poor maintenance. If not replaced soon, at about $13, the entire saddle will deteriorate. New saddle: $35.

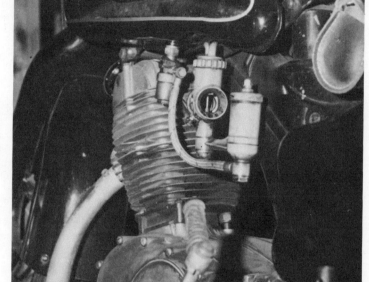

An air cleaner is missing from this carburetor. It should be replaced to prevent excessive engine wear. It is also a fire hazard from any engine backfire.

18 on the rear wheel. On a big machine the front tire runs around $17-18 and the rear one about $20. Japanese tires may be less expensive generally, but Dunlop, Avon, and Pirelli tires appear to last longer. A small tire will, of course, wear faster than a big one. And fast take-offs and sudden stops reduce tire life.

Under no circumstances try to change the tire(s) yourself. The dealer will probably charge about $2 per tire for mounting it on the wheel and it's well worth the money. Mounting a motorcycle tire requires infinite care and experience. Even the best mechanics pinch tubes with the tire levers occasionally. That's why they charge so much—they have to make allowance for pinched tubes that are replaced at the dealer's expense. Unlike automobile mechanics, they have no machines to make the job easier. If it's a competition bike with

security bolts, expect to pay extra. They're more trouble.

When you've inspected the tires take a close look at the wheels. Are all the spokes in place, straight, and tight? Is the rim true and undented? Are spokes and rim free of rust? Looking will reveal the answers to all these questions but one. To test the rim for trueness (see photo) hold a screwdriver tip close to the side of the rim, brace your hand on the fender and rotate the wheel with the bike on its center stand. The distance between screwdriver tip and rim should not vary as the wheel turns.

If you take a wheel off and remove tire and spokes yourself it costs about $15 to have a wheel respoked. If you need a new rim as well, this adds another $15 or so. If the wheel wobbles, but not too badly, it can often be trued up by a dealer without replacing any parts. With tire removed he can put it in a jig and adjust the tension on the spokes to restore balance. The labor charge depends on how long this takes.

Brakes

There's only one sure way to determine brake lining wear: take off the wheels and look at the linings. Since this isn't likely, the next best test is to try them on the road at highway speeds. Pushing the bike by hand and clamping on the brakes proves nothing since comparatively little stopping power is required.

A telltale sign will indicate if the brake linings are definitely worn badly, but the absence of that sign won't prove anything. Specifically, if the front brake arm (on single-leading-shoe brakes) makes a right angle with the brake cable and the rear brake arm makes a right angle with the brake rod there is virtually no adjustment left (see photo). Not only have the linings been worn thin, there is less mechanical advantage available to activate the brake shoes.

The angles between brake arms and cable or rod may be less than 90°—as on a new bike—without indicating the presence of new linings, however. Both brake arms can be removed from their serrated shafts and replaced in a new position, to get a fresh "bite." The angles will then suggest a lining thickness that doesn't exist; but it will also restore the original mechanical advantage. This procedure, therefore, is not necessarily carried out to deceive anyone, but simply to get the last bit of use from worn brakes.

The odometer reading may be some help, if it's accurate. Many small machines go indefinitely without needing new brake linings—weight and speed are relatively low. On a large machine like a Triumph you can expect 15,000 miles or more on a set of brakes; a BMW gets about 20,000 miles. Most riders wear out the rear brake faster because they use it more.

A competition bike may wear out its brakes much faster than this because water, sand and mud get on the linings and wear or deteriorate them. Sometimes a lining will get soggy and lose its grip, despite adequate thickness. Such linings should be replaced, since it's the performance of a brake that counts, not its appearance.

A soggy brake can also mean some grease from the wheel bearing has leaked past the seal and spread onto the brake drum to be picked up by the linings. No amount of cleaning with gasoline or roughening with sandpaper or a file will fully restore the stopping power of such a lining. So when in doubt about the effectiveness of a bike's brakes, plan to replace them.

Another good reason for this policy is that if the linings have been worn down far enough to expose the tops of the rivets (if linings are fastened to the shoes with rivets rather than by bonding) the rivets will score the drums. Then the drums should be turned down to get a smooth surface again, otherwise they'll score the new linings and accelerate wear.

Again, if you take the wheel off and put it back on, the dealer will replace linings on a large bike like a Triumph for only $3 per wheel. If he has to take the wheel off and replace it the price goes up to about $5. Some dealers, like Slegers Company, send your original shoes to a specialist who removes the old linings and bonds new ones on. Bonded shoes are better, since there's more lining material in contact with the drums and you can wear them down farther without danger of scoring the drums with rivet heads.

Steering

The steering-head bearing is the most likely trouble spot in the steering system. There are two tests you can use to determine its condition. First, to test for excessive play, pull down on the front fork legs (see photo). Turn the front wheel from side to side—if there's no resistance at all to turning there is too much play.

Second, grip the front fender with one hand and feel the edge of the steering-head bearing with the other (see photo). Move the wheel from side to side—the steering head should turn smoothly. If it moves unevenly, as though over a rough surface, the bearing balls have worn depressions in the races so that they "lock into" the low places.

It may be possible to cure excessive play by tightening up on the adjusting nut above the bearing. But if this doesn't work, or if the races have been dented by the balls, you'll need a new set of races. This could cost as much as $30. New bearing balls, if needed, cost pennies.

Handlebars also affect steering, so look them over for damage—usually caused by dropping the machine and bending one side. Even new bars in perfect shape can be unacceptable if their design is extreme. "Ape hangers" are now illegal in some states; they're unsafe everywhere. If the bike has these monstrosities ask the owner to replace them with the originals, if he still has them. Or allow $5 to $15, the price for a new pair on most makes and sizes. Allow several dollars more for installation if you don't plan to disconnect all the controls and cables from the old ones yourself.

Suspension

Springs seldom wear out or break in the front and rear suspensions of road machines. Trouble usually comes in the oil damping system that controls the rebound of the multirate springs inside the suspension units. Oil oozes past the seals and appears where the upper and lower covers of the unit overlap. It usually picks up road dust and is visible as a black streak, spread downward by the telescoping motion of the suspension. Even brand new machines of some makes show such leakage from the front forks.

This makes it tough to tell just what shape a front suspension is in. Jouncing the front end up and down by the handlebars won't tell you much—the owner may even have drained all the oil out. A test ride is the only practical way to find out. Slide the rubber boots, if any, up out of the way and wipe any oil off the lower half of the suspension unit. Then take a ride of three or four miles. If the oil was drained out, the forks will "bottom" on bumps with a clacking noise as metal strikes metal; the ride will be on the rough side, too. When the ride's over, if there is oil in the same place as before, you will at least need new oil seals. This requires the forks to be dismantled, a considerable amount of labor that varies according to machine.

If you find considerable oil leakage from a rear suspension unit you will have to replace the entire unit, since these are sealed "for life." Each unit could cost as much as $18. Labor is low because they're easy to replace.

Again the odometer and some generalizations may help you decide whether the suspension is too far gone. A medium-weight bike is good for at least 20,000 miles without attention, unless it's been roughly used. Japanese front ends appear to require little attention, while the front forks of British machines need watching. A machine that has had few front-fork oil changes or has been stored in an unheated place, where moisture has condensed inside, is a poor risk.

Controls and Instruments

Most motorcycle controls are connected to the handlebar, so let's start there. Bear in mind that the feel of some controls depends not only on the lever itself but the condition of the device it operates. This inspection should focus on the controls themselves.

Clutch and front brake controls are the principal ones. Are the levers firmly attached, unbroken and unbent, easy to reach (some are adjustable, some not)? Are the cable covers intact, do they fit tightly against the lever unit, do they lead neatly through clips? Does lever movement have an immediate effect or does it require considerable movement to affect clutch or brake? Is there room left to adjust effective cable length?

Bent or broken levers, cables that are frayed or stretched beyond adjustment, cable covers that are bent or partially broken will have to be replaced. None of these parts is expensive and they can be replaced by the average rider. Slack cables and cable covers that hang loosely can easily be adjusted and clipped in place, respectively.

You can check the choke lever (if any), spark advance (if any), and ignition "kill"

Chain guard was removed here, exposing the chain to water and dirt. Replacing guard can cost $10-15, but is urged for safety.

button (if any) when you ride the bike.

Assuming the motorcycle has a battery, turn on the headlight and tail light, operate the high/low beam switch, try the brake light switch, and blow the horn. If the machine's electrical system uses a magneto or energy-transfer system you'll have to start the bike up to make these tests. If there's supposed to be a battery, but isn't, you won't be able to test until one is connected. Don't buy without testing—all kinds of expensive things could be wrong, as explained under Electrical System.

If the bike has an ammeter you can tell whether it's working by turning on the lights when the engine's not running. The needle should swing over to the minus side of zero. Then when the bike is started up the needle should swing over to the plus side of zero. Otherwise, of course, the needle should point to zero—unless the movement has been damaged or there is a low-grade short somewhere that's draining the battery. A new ammeter sells for $2-4.

The speedometer and its cable deserve careful examination. If it doesn't register during the road test, unscrew the cable housing from the underside of the speedometer head and hold the cable end between thumb and forefinger. If the speedometer is driven off the front wheel, spin that wheel with the machine on its center stand. If driven off the back wheel, spin that wheel. If driven off the engine or transmission, run the bike on the stand briefly. Grasp the cable end firmly enough so that it twists in your fingers; if it doesn't twist the cable is broken inside the housing and will have to be replaced for $8-10, including labor. Sometimes a disconnected cable will rotate because the two jagged ends, at the break, mesh well enough to turn just the cable. But the force required to drive the speedometer mechanism is too much for such a loose connection.

If the speedo cable is all right and there was no registration of speed or mileage during your test ride, the fault lies with the speedometer head. Unless it can be fixed—and there are specialists who do repairs on these instruments—it will cost up to $24 for a new one. You can easily install one yourself.

Electrical System

You've already gotten some idea of the shape the electrical system is in by checking for missing parts and trying light switches A new battery will cost $11-28 depending on size—you already know whether you'll need one. The Japanese batteries appear to perform well.

Its tread worn off, this tire is unsafe. Bracing hand against fender, mechanic holds screwdriver blade close to turning wheel to test rim trueness.

If the bike has an ammeter and you tested it by starting the engine, you already know whether the generator is working: a plus indication shows the generator is charging and a minus indication shows it's not. Failure to charge may be the fault of the voltage regulator (if there is one) or the rectifier. Or it could be generator trouble. Any of these troubles can be expensive, not only in new parts but in trouble-shooting time, since electrical troubles are notoriously tricky. A regulator or rectifier can easily exceed $12-14 while an alternator or generator can run $20-40.

Now take a close look at all the electrical wires. Many of those running between the ignition switch and handlebar will be bundled inside a rubber sleeve as an added protection. Is the sleeve intact, especially where it passes the front downtube or steering head, or has it been chafed through on the inner side? Has the sleeve deteriorated so that the wires are straggling in a loose bunch, some of them worn badly? If so it could cost up to $35 to rewire the bike. Some riders fancy themselves electricians and have their own improvised wiring, which may be asking for trouble with shorts or an overloaded circuit.

Some British-made machines in the early 1960's were just getting started with alternators and had problems disposing of extra electricity generated during daylight hours when no lights were needed. In recent years this has been solved by adding a "zener diode" that converts the extra juice into heat which is dissipated into the air. Be cautious, therefore, about older British bikes—ask what kind of voltage regulation or current dissipation system it has.

Engine

The single most important part of the bike, of course, is the engine. It's especially true of this part of the machine that you can't really be sure of its condition without taking it completely apart. So you'll have to collect a series of impressions, adding them up to see whether there are so many deficiencies that it's best to pass up the bike entirely or whether the defects are minor and inexpensively remedied.

How about the exhaust pipes? If they're heavily blued it could mean that the fuel-air mixture has been too lean—in which case the exhaust valves and seats may be burned. Or the machine might have been left running on its stand, which usually does no harm to the engine. Or the pipe may be made of thin metal, poorly chromed, which again means the engine has not been harmed. Or the bike may be a single-cylinder four-stroke; they commonly blue their pipes harmlessly because of greater-than-average valve overlap.

But blued pipes could also signal a hard-pressed engine—one that's been run near its limit continually either by a road or a competition rider. If the air cleaner is missing and the pipe has megaphone exhausts it was probably raced. Buying one of these would be courting expensive trouble, like buying a used taxicab. If only appearance bothers you, expect to pay up to $16 for a new pipe.

Then, is there an air cleaner attached to the carburetor? Every modern machine has one. Some riders take them off because they've heard that performance is better without one. This may have been true some time ago, but is true no longer. Modern paper and plastic-foam air cleaners pass much larger volumes of air than the older kind. Not only is removing the air cleaner a wasted effort, it exposes the engine to greater wear from airborne dirt and makes the machine more vulnerable to fire if there is a backfire through the carburetor. Bikes have been totally destroyed by a backfire that ignited the saddle above the carburetor and then spread. So if there's no air cleaner put down an-

other minus and expect to spend $5-10 for a new one if you buy the machine anyway.

Next, feel around the top of the crankcase where the cylinders are spigotted into it. If you find oil there you'll have to decide whether the leak is serious enough to keep the machine looking sloppy, or using more oil than average. One way to find out is to wipe the top of the crankcase clean with a rag before your test ride and then check again for further leakage after the ride. If leakage is extensive it will cost $35-40 to have the barrels removed so that a seal costing about a quarter can be replaced.

Of course if you expect to have some top-end work done anyway—pistons, rings, valves, and so on—then you'll have to pay that kind of labor charge anyway. Actually, little or no harm is done to the engine by such an oil leak; it's a matter of appearance and heavier oil consumption.

Take a look at the ignition points next. You'll have to remove a cover plate to get at them. Their condition will tell you a good deal about the health of the ignition system and the habits of the owner. They should be clean and have smooth faces with adequate tungsten (the gray metal) still there. Dirt, pitted or uneven faces and broken parts indicate poor maintenance. Severe pitting (a hole in one face, a mound on the other) could mean arcing caused by condenser or coil problems. The points

Right angle between rear brake arm and brake rod indicates brake adjustment has been used up. The screwdriver shows arm angle when shoes are new.

Pushing the forks up and down tests the front end for undesirable play in the motorcycle. Movement means a loose steering head or worn fork bushings.

Condition of steering head is tested by turning wheel and feeling steering head bearing for worn spots in races. Movement should always be smooth.

themselves are inexpensive, but should probably be put in by a mechanic and properly gapped if you're inexperienced.

Spark plugs are an excellent indicator of carburetion. Both electrodes should be intact and either a light brown or gray. If they're black, then the fuel-air mixture is set too rich, reducing performance and increasing gas consumption. Or black plugs could indicate that lubricating oil is getting past the oil rings on the pistons and

being burned in the combustion chamber. White electrodes, sometimes burned away in places, indicate a lean mixture. This produces a very hot flame in the combustion chamber that may warp or burn exhaust valves and seats. It's the worst sign of the three and ties in with a blued exhaust pipe.

While you have the spark plugs out it's a good time to check compression with a compression gauge. This is the single most valuable test of a used engine because it tells you whether the piston rings are still tight and the valves properly seated. If the combustion chamber can hold air under great pressure it will drive the piston down with maximum energy and produce maximum power output. If air leaks out past rings and valves the energy is dissipated and performance suffers.

You can buy your own compression gauge in an auto supply store or mail order house for about $5. It's probably worth buying one because you can use it later to keep your own bike in top shape. The markings are in pounds per square inch. You take a reading by holding the gauge tightly in the spark plug hole and pushing down on the kickstarter until that cylinder is on its compression stroke (see photo). It may take two people—one to hold the gauge, the other to work the kickstarter; *you* hold the gauge.

If the gauge shows 150 pounds or over, the cylinder is in good shape. If it reads under 100 pounds there is trouble. Low compression could be caused by a valve that's adjusted too tightly or by loose (worn) rings. A good way, to find out which, is to squirt a small amount of oil into the cylinder through the spark plug hole so that it coats the rings. Then check compression again with the gauge. If it shoots way up, say from 60 to 150, the trouble is worn rings. If compression goes up only a little the trouble is probably valves. The oil acts as a seal, making up for the loose fit.

Low compression always means money. Replacing just the rings costs $6-7 in parts for the average bike and another $35 for labor. If the cylinder needs reboring (from being worn out of round) add another $16. Pistons run $3-8 for a small bike and $15-20 for a medium-to-large bike. Valves add as much as $7 for each exhaust valve, $5-6 for each intake valve. Valve springs cost about $9 a set and valve guides are another $8 per cylinder. Cutting valve seats and facing the new valves adds another $5. So it's expensive.

Wires have been stretched and abraded where they bend around the front of frame. This is a likely trouble spot and can cause intermittent shorts.

Pipes are heavily blued on this motorcycle, either from hard riding, lean carburetor mixture or letting the machine idle too long at rest.

Think twice before you decide to buy a bike with low compression. A motorcycle operates close to its performance limit most of the time; lose half its power and you haven't got much left. It's more serious than buying a used car that's not up to scratch, for example.

You can't tell much more without starting up the engine. The carburetor may be dirty on the outside but this tells you nothing. You may be able to shove a stick up the mufflers without striking anything, but this also means nothing. Many modern mufflers have the sound-absorbing element placed concentrically around the perimeter of the muffler rather than in the center. The old night-stick-in-the-exhaust is no longer a valid test.

To a pro who has heard dozens of engines and know the healthy sound of each make, the second most useful test is listening to engine noises. You may not be as experienced, but there are some obvious things to beware of.

Start the engine, let it warm up, then set the throttle for idle. Stuff rags in the exhaust pipes to cut down the exhaust note and get your ears close to the engine. An aluminum-alloy engine will make more noise, of course, than an iron-barrelled one. But excessive thumping, rattling, knocking, or hammering is bad news. You can develop your sense of what's "excessive" by listening to a bike of the same make and model in good shape beforehand.

If the engine sounds all right at idle, turn up the wick a little and listen again. Do some more listening with the throttle turned all the way off until the engine almost stalls. The noises are sometimes different at these other throttle settings, which can tell you more.

Excessive noise, like low compression, means expensive trouble. Here again it's best not to take chances; cross the bike off your list.

While you've got the bike running you can get some hint of carburetor condition. With the engine idling, open the throttle briskly, as you would when accelerating. If pickup is slow or the engine stalls—provided it's warmed up—there may be carburetor trouble. Poor ignition can also cause this, so the test isn't definitive for a bad carburetor. Make sure you've pulled the rags out of the mufflers before you perform the last test.

With the rags out listen to the exhaust note, outdoors. A loud one may get you in trouble with the police or actually cause pain on a long trip. If the muffler has been "gutted" (the silencing element removed) or a nonstandard straight pipe has been substituted for the original equipment, you'll spend $10-30 for each new one.

You're foolish to ride with anything but an original-equipment muffler, not only because it's legal and less irritating to yourself and the public, but because it was designed to go with that particular engine. Two-strokes in particular need exactly the right amount of expansion space and back pressure to get maximum performance. By removing or changing the exhaust pipe and muffler you probably will actually hurt performance, not help it.

Comparison of old and new sprockets shows how the teeth become hooked by worn chain. The upper sprocket is new, while the lower is well worn.

Transmission System

The gearbox is sealed; you will have to guess the condition of the gears by performance tests rather than physical appearance. But you *can* see the rear drive chain and sprocket.

The chain should be slightly moist with lubricant, not dry. And it should look tight without looking taut; nor should it hang down in the center of the lower run. Don't be put off if the rear chain is completely enclosed. Though protected better from road dirt, an enclosed chain can also become loose from stretching and run dry, unnoticed. Normally a chain is good for 10,000 miles and a rear-wheel sprocket is good for 25,000 miles. Japanese chains appear to wear faster than British Renold chains. Spanish chains appear to wear the fastest of any.

If all you need is a new chain the bill will amount to $6-14. But look closely at the rear-wheel sprocket too; if the teeth are hooked (see photo) it may cost another $30 to put on a new one. Even the engine sprocket may be badly worn—another $8-15 for parts and labor. If you replace a bad chain without replacing worn sprockets you'll quickly ruin the new chain and any successors.

The gears can be tested in two ways, with the bike on its stand, and out on the road. With the machine on its center stand, put it successively in each gear and move the rear wheel to test for excessive play. Allow for slack in the drive chain, of course. On the road pay particular attention to the crispness, or lack of it, with which you can make shifts. Then as a further test, put the bike in second and goose it (give it throttle suddenly). If the dogs in the gearbox have been rounded by wear, the machine will pop out of gear.

This sequence of tests will also give you some idea of the clutch's condition. It should not slip or grab. A new clutch, if that's all that's needed, will run $5-10 for parts and $10 or more for labor. It may be that only an adjustment is needed, but don't take chances, allow for a new clutch.

New gears are expensive and so is the labor. If they're really bad it's probably not worth bothering with the bike. It may even be impossible to get new gears and shafts for old machines. And riding with gears that pop out can be dangerous on the highway.

General Advice

Don't be afraid to buy a machine that's been laid up— as long as it has been stored in a heated place. If everything else is satisfactory, clean out the carburetor, drain and replace the oil, check the battery for water, examine the tires for dry rot and pump them up. Be sure the seals (gaskets) haven't dried out completely. That's all it takes.

A bike that's been stored in an unheated garage or basement, however, probably has begun to rust inside the engine and suspension units from condensed moisture. The pistons may have seized, gas tank be rusting inside, carburetor completely gummed up, and so on.

Anyone who puts down several hundred dollars for a used machine without riding it, say the pros, is a nut. And no reputable dealer (or rider) will deny that right to a prospective buyer with a proper driver's license and clothing (including safety helmet where required). They suggest, however, that a prospective buyer should not take off, for an hour, out of sight of the shop. They can't tell whether he's made off with the machine permanently or is lying injured on some poorly traveled road. Ride back and forth 50 times in front of the shop, if you like, but don't stretch things too far.

Take a knowledgeable friend along if you want. But be sure he's knowledgeable —it takes several years for even an alert rider to gain experience. Some people, of course, never learn, but are always willing to give advice. So know your man.

The safest way to buy a used machine is always to find a good dealer you can trust. He'll tell you what he's done to fix up the bike and give you a guarantee for a limited mileage, or time. It doesn't pay to match wits with a dealer you can't trust— he's way ahead of any amateur.

Finally, add up the cost of fixing any machine you're interested in. Then add this total to the purchase price. If the sum of the two is more than a hundred dollars it may be better to spend that on a newer bike that's already in good shape. Unless you're a collector of antiques, it doesn't pay to sink much money in repairs just to end up with an old machine from which you can never get back the repair bill, either in personal use or resale value. Unfortunately, it costs as much to fix a very old machine as it does to fix a brand new one. Be sure you're not throwing good money after bad.

Now you *know* why Jack Creelman says "one of the most miserable things in the world to buy is a used motorcycle." It's a selfish warning. No one who's in motorcycling for fun or business wants to see a beginning rider give up in disgust because of a bad experience with a used machine. •

Lewis Buchanan, right, explains use of reflecting tape on motorcycles and rider's clothing to Robert Rudy, left, of M.S. & A.T.A., and Mac McGarry, center, of NBC-TV. The three appear in "You Can Prevent Accidents," a TV program. Buchanan is acting chief of Motorcycle Div., National Highway Safety Bureau.

Safety

THANKS to Ralph Nader, motor vehicle safety is on everyone's mind; because of 2,000 fatalities a year, motorcyclists have become clearly visible as a group of road users to be specially protected.

Few people, Americans especially, like to be told how to protect themselves. It automatically galvanizes them into writing letters to their legislators, arguing their constitutional rights in court, and writing indignant magazine articles. This is not such a piece.

The cold fact is that we already have a great many more safety regulations in effect aimed especially at motorcyclists than we have ever had in our history. An even colder prediction is that we will have

a great many more—and soon. A corollary prediction is that these regulations will eventually become reasonably uniform throughout the country and that by and large they will be good ones.

At this late date there is really little purpose served by beating our breasts over a point that is no longer moot. Despite some half-dozen cases being argued in as many states over whether it's constitutional to require a motorcycle rider to wear an approved safety helmet, in the broadest sense safety has been accepted as a legitimate concern of government. We wouldn't have pasteurized milk, government-inspected meat, restrictions on the sale of drugs, regulations controlling the actions of ships and aircraft, and so on if this were not so.

The Federal Program

The motive force behind the sudden rash of motorcycle safety regulations is

Department of Transportation can slice 10% off any federal highway construction funds earmarked for that state.

It is an unprecedented weapon to be placed in the hands of safety experts. What the National Highway Safety Bureau does, therefore, is undoubtedly more important in the long run than any public relations campaign mounted by national or local organizations representing importers, manufacturers, dealers, or motorcyclists. This is not to say that such campaigns will have no effect, simply that their influence will be minor in comparison with the impact of direct, powerful federal intervention.

What, then, are the federal safety administrators up to? So far they have issued some specific and some general "criteria standards" in 13 areas. One area is motorcycle safety and it's currently under the immediate supervision of Lewis S. Buchanan, acting chief of the Motorcycle Safety Division in the National Highway Safety Bureau of the new U.S. Department of Transportation.

Mr. Buchanan, a youngish man who rides a mediumweight Yamaha and competes in sportsman events on weekends,

more than just idle concern or malice. What powers the drive is the federal purse, an increasingly potent influence as state problems outgrow the capabilities of state treasuries.

More specifically, section 402c of the Highway Safety Act of 1966, enacted by the 89th Congress, says: "Use of Funds. After December 31, 1968, the Secretary shall not apportion any funds under this sub-section to any state which is not implementing a highway safety program approved by the Secretary in accordance with this section. Federal aid highway funds apportioned on or after January 1, 1969 to any state which is not implementing a highway safety program approved by the Secretary in accordance with this section shall be reduced by amounts equal to 10 percentum of the amounts which would otherwise be apportioned to such state under section 104 of this title, until such time as such state is implementing an approved highway safety program."

It doesn't require a law degree to translate this into simpler language: If a state doesn't put into effect the safety regulations proposed by the National Highway Safety Bureau, the secretary of the U.S.

The dramatic effect of reflectorized tape is apparent on motorcycle, at left. Bike, on right, has no tape, to demonstrate the contrast. Tape reportedly makes the rider visible at a distance of 1,000 feet.

Straight pipes substituted for original equipment, on this 650 twin Triumph, may be safety in reverse. His presence is painfully apparent to other motorists, not all of whom will appreciate rider's artistic effort.

moved over to his present spot from the Division of Accident Prevention in the U.S. Public Health Service. In conversation he is friendly, helpful, and apparently committed to a gradual, cautious enactment of safety standards for motorcycle riders and their machines.

So far Mr. Buchanan's division has issued one such standard for motorcycles. Dated June 27, 1967, it explains the reason for the standard, defines a motorcycle, and advises states to: examine and license drivers of motorcycles, require motorcycle operators and passengers to wear "approved" safety helmets, require a seat and footrests for each passenger carried on a motorcycle, require each bike to have a rear-view mirror, and require an annual inspection of every motorcycle according to state requirements.

Manual Will Spell Out Rules

Now under review by top administrators and lawyers of the National Highway Safety Bureau is a draft manual with five parts or chapters: (1) Motorcycle Safety Standards, (2) Motorcycle—Operator Licensing, (3) Motorcycle—Personal Protective Equipment, (4) Motorcycle—Vehicle Equipment, and (5) Motorcycle—Vehicle Inspection.

Seven members of an *ad hoc* committee advised Buchanan on the draft manual. Paul L. McCrillis, director of governmental relations for the Motorcycle, Scooter and Allied Trades Association was one. The others represented the American Driver and Traffic Safety Education Association, the American Automobile Association, the American Association of Motor Vehicle Administrators, the International

Before members of American Association of Motor Vehicle Administrators, Cliff Guild demonstrates the pylon-cone course recommended as part of a model exam by Motorcycle, Scooter and Allied Trades Assoc.

Association of Chiefs of Police, the U.S. Public Health Service, and an association of insurance companies.

The draft manual will spell out in greater detail the recommendations made in 1967. Expectations in the Bureau are that the draft manual will be released for publication about July 1, 1968 but no one is willing to make a firm prediction. Nor is it certain yet whether these standards will be characterized as "guidelines" or "requirements."

Buchanan and his fellow safety administrators in the National Highway Safety Bureau freely admit that a great deal of research needs to be done into accidents, vehicle and road design, and driver behavior before they will know enough to write well-grounded standards. This will take considerable time and money, so their strategy is to base present standards on what is known or suspected so far — on the grounds that some action is better than none. Then as research provides solid information they'll modify the standards, if necessary, to reflect improved knowledge.

There is no question about the value of driver licensing, annual vehicle inspection, and the wearing of such safety gear as a helmet and eye protection. What's not clear yet to Buchanan is what performance standards should be applied to safety helmets. Nor is he sure about the wisdom of some safety devices for motorcycles — like crash bars for lightweight machines.

Research Planned

One aspect of the safety research will be creation of an accident-investigation team along the lines of the Federal Aviation Agency teams that unravel the causes of airplane crashes. Following another track, the National Traffic Safety Institute (a unit of the National Highway Safety Bureau) is already collecting published information on highway accidents.

The deliberate, thorough, compassionate approach apparently being made by the federal safety administrators suggest that highway safety regulation is here to stay and that it will be intelligently handled.

What We Can Do

Does this mean we should all fold up our concerns and let them fade away into the night now that Big Uncle has arrived on the scene? By no means, for two reasons. One is that every administrator works better under the constant scrutiny of his knowledgeable "clients." The other is that there are some worthwhile things all of us can do in order to harvest the greatest return from a laudable effort:

• State safety administrators, from the governor down, should know that three highly placed federal officials have each publicly declared that "compliance" with the existing safety standards will be liberally interpreted. Any progress toward adoption and implementation of them, even appointing a commission or committee to set up a state safety apparatus where there is none, will be considered acceptable. Only if a state refuses point blank to take any action will it be penalized, the officials have suggested.

This assurance and the Bureau's own caution in adopting standards carry a strong message: states need not be in a hurry to take action. Nor should they be if it will mean hasty and ill-advised "implementation" that violates the spirit of the federal standards. A plea of necessity cannot honestly be used to rush through state regulations that punish rather than protect motorcyclists.

CONTROLS ON 20 MOTORCYCLES

Model	Clutch Lever	Shift Lever	Shift Pattern	Front Brake Lever	Rear Brake Pedal
Benelli 250 Barracuda	LH	RF	B	RH	LF
Bridgestone 175 Hurricane	LH	LF	C	RH	RF
BSA Starfire 250	LH	RF	A	RH	LF
BMW R 69 S	LH	LF	A	RH	RF
Bultaco Metrella 250	LH	RF	B	RH	LF
CZ 250 Trials	LH	LF	B	RH	RF
Greeves Anglian 246	LH	RF	B	RH	LF
Harley-Davidson Sprint	LH	RF	A	RH	LF
Sportster	LH	RF	A	RH	LF
FLH	LH	LF	A	RH	RF
Honda 160	LH	LF	A	RH	RF
Husqvarna 360	LH	RF	A	RH	LF
Jawa 350	LH	LF	B	RH	RF
Kawasaki 350	LH	LF	D	RH	RF
Montesa 250	LH	RF	A	RH	LF
Norton 750	LH	RF	B	RH	LF
Ossa 230	LH	LF	A	RH	RF
Suzuki X5	LH	LF	A	RH	RF
Triumph T100 R	LH	RF	A	RH	LF
Yamaha 350	LH	LF	A	RH	RF

Key to Shift Patterns

A Down for first	B Up for first	C Top neutral	D Bottom neutral
Up to neutral, second, third, etc.	Down to neutral, second, third, etc.	Down for all speeds	Up for all speeds

A second important implication is that states would be wise to establish legislative or administrative machinery at the outset that permits revisions in their standards from time to time, as research findings alter federal recommendations.

One standard is uncertain and promises to remain so for some time. This is the performance standard for safety helmets. For some reason the Motorcycle, Scooter and Allied Trades Association (the motorcycle industry's trade association) persists in urging states to adopt its one-blow standard for helmets, and many states have done so. The Z90 Committee of the United States of America Standards Institute, after deliberating four years, recommended a two-blow standard and other states have adopted that.

The Z90.1 standard was intended to apply only to competition; it's unnecessarily stiff for street riding, says the M.S. & A.T.A. If you're going to wear a helmet at all, why not wear the best protection you can get? the Snell Memorial Foundation and others respond. Significantly, the Safety Helmet Council of America (an association of helmet makers) has officially endorsed the Z90.1 two-blow standard.

[The blows referred to are carefully specified in the standards and their effect on the helmet's shell and contents (an instrumented head form) is electronically measured. The two-blow standard requires a helmet to perform satisfactorily under the impact of two test blows in succession on exactly the same spot. The one-blow standard requires only half that capability.]

The squabble over helmet standards has gone on for several years during the critical period when many states have been struggling with the new, unfamiliar safety problem. The result: a split from coast to coast. It would be a kindness to everyone, including the M.S. & A.T.A., if it joined the side of the angels.

• Then there is something manufacturers can do. They can come closer to a standard control pattern. As the chart Controls on 20 Motorcycles shows, there is universal agreement in placing the clutch lever on the left handlebar and the front brake lever on the right handlebar. But from there on it's every man for himself. Shift lever and rear brake pedal are split down the middle, with half the machines carrying their shift levers on the left side and half carrying them on the right. Though 12 bikes use shift pattern A —down for first, then up to neutral, second, third, and fourth—there are three other patterns among the remaining eight motorcycles.

It used to be a quaint game when Indian and Harley-Davidson had their hand-shift levers on opposite sides and foot clutches that worked opposite to one another. It kept me off Harley-Davidsons because I didn't trust my reflexes in an emergency. Some close calls while testing a wide range of motorcycles and scooters has amply confirmed the danger.

With over 2,000,000 riders in the sport here—and no one knows how many more elsewhere in the world—we can no longer afford the luxury of ignoring this hazard. It's not only good safety but good business to offer two-wheel customers the same uniformity they take for granted in cars.

• Dealers could help by refusing to sell accessories that are dangerous or have a high public-nuisance value. "Ape hangers" (high-curving handlebars) fall in the first category and straight pipes fall in the second. Most experienced riders will agree that such odd-ball accessories as "ape hangers," low-slung saddles, missing fenders, "sissy bars" (a high-rising bar curving around behind the saddle) are dangerous. What many riders fail to realize is that raucous exhausts, weird accessories and clothing—to say nothing of wild riding—are also dangerous because they create hostility in many automobile drivers. I've run across too many drivers who have gone so far around the bend on motorcyclists that they're consciously out to scare, injure, or kill us. There are even more who are so inclined semi-consciously.

• Those in the business of renting motorcycles could do everyone a favor by going out of business unless they are in a state with motorcycle operators' licenses. To send complete tyros out onto the public highways with no more than five minutes instruction is an act of outrageous optimism or of callous greed.

• Riders can follow the rules of the road and common sense. Then, with clean hands, we can insist that car drivers do the same. Sure, better-equipped motorcycles and better wearing apparel will help reduce accidents. But 20 years of riding have convinced me that motorcyclists are primarily victims of the pecking order. Trucks avoid clanging with buses, cars avoid trucks, little cars avoid big ones, and no vehicle is smaller than a motorcycle. "I just didn't notice it, officer" is one of the most familiar statements in motorcycle accident reports.

For all of us, now is the time to raise our eyes from individual concerns and focus simultaneously on the common goal of reducing a tragic toll. As civilized people we can do no less than our best.

This demonstration of right-angle parking, in New York City, launched the MCA. It proved to officials that it makes much better sense to park two-wheelers at right angles to the curb than parallel to it.

MCA... The Motorcyclist's Triple A

DISCRIMINATORY legislation and careless administrators brought the country's nine automobile clubs together in Chicago on March 4, 1902. They agreed to affiliate as the American Automobile Association and fight zealous but ignorant lawmakers on a nationwide basis.

Today, of course, no one would dare close public parks to four-wheeled vehicles, or impose a five-mile-per-hour speed limit on them, or refuse to recognize an out-of-state driver's license. There are 11 million AAA members and they speak with a mighty voice through their representatives.

Motorcycle riders find themselves somewhat in the same position as automobile drivers did 66 years ago. Some public

The campaign did bring eight motorcycle-only parking areas, this one on Broadway near 59th Street. All the parking areas are heavily used.

Traffic Commissioner Barnes says he does not approve of angle parking because of danger of damage in accidents. Cyclists argue they're no better off in parallel parking and claim it takes up twice as much room.

parks and highways carry "No Motorcycles Allowed" signs at their entrances. A Brooklyn legislator wants to put 35 mph governors on two wheelers, and some states won't recognize the helmets approved by others.

Two New Yorkers have seen the parallel and begun doing something. It started innocently enough on June 28, 1966, when Ralph Lao rallied 100 motorcycle and scooter owners on Park Avenue. His aim was to prove to New York City officials, through the press and TV, that it makes much better sense to park two-wheelers at right angles to the curb than parallel to it. The demonstration proved that you could pack all 100 in a single city block—about four two-wheeled vehicles in the space required by one car.

Lao, president of a textbook illustrating firm, got 200 phone calls after the demonstration. Besides parking, New Yorkers said they were worried about the high cost of insurance, rising thefts of two-wheelers, helmet laws. The American Motorcycle Association and its local clubs were doing very little, Lao decided, and there was no other organization to be a Triple A for riders. So he organized the Metropolitan Cycle Association, with himself as president and his partner in the illustrating firm, Kathleen Tyler, as secretary.

Less than two years have gone by and the results are impressive. Already, some 3,500 metropolitan New Yorkers have put up $10 or $20 to join (the lower dues figure for regular membership and the higher one for so-called VIP membership with special benefits). Files, desks, and a waiting area for MCA have pushed Ralph and Kathy's textbook illustrating business into a back room. They haven't been able to spend full time on MCA yet, except during the summer. But they have one full-time and two part-time men handling pickups of disabled cycles with a panel truck. Another part-timer handles cycle riding instruction.

Pickups of members' bikes now run about 100 a month on the average. During the summer of 1967 their instructor taught about 100 new riders on their dual-control Honda. The demand for driver training exceeds the instructor's available time.

Among the other things MCA has done is offer a key-return service, discounts on merchandise (except motorcycles) at cooperating dealers, establishment of a motorcycle unit within the auto theft squad of New York's police department, the setting up of eight motorcycle-only parking areas between Wall Street and 59th Street in Manhattan, bike rides for kids to a ball game, appearances on two network TV programs, publication of a small newspaper for members, and numerous appearances at public meetings to represent the motorcyclists' point of view.

MCA has run some week-end tours to the nearby countryside and one two-day trip to Puerto Rico. It hopes to launch an annual tour of Europe on motorcycles during the summer of 1969. It would also like to offer a general travel service and is investigating new sources of two-wheel vehicle insurance that will cut premiums down to size.

Ironically, the issue that propelled Ralph Lao and Kathy Tyler into founding a motorcycle equivalent of the Triple A is still unsettled, despite numerous demonstrations, letters, and personal appearances. The villain, apparently, is Traffic Commissioner Henry Barnes who confessed to a reporter that he hasn't trusted motorcycles since he fell off one at the impressionable age of 18—while waving to a girl. Commissioner Barnes is now 60, which shows how long a lesson can last with some people. And his personal bias has determined New York City policy, despite direct appeals to Mayor John Lindsay.

Bike-a-Kid-to-the-Ballpark was a big success. It brought more than 200 riders and children together from all parts of New York City for a cyclecade to Yankee Stadium baseball game. There were no accidents, everyone had fun, and, for a change, cyclists received good notices. Typical of happy participants were two, left.

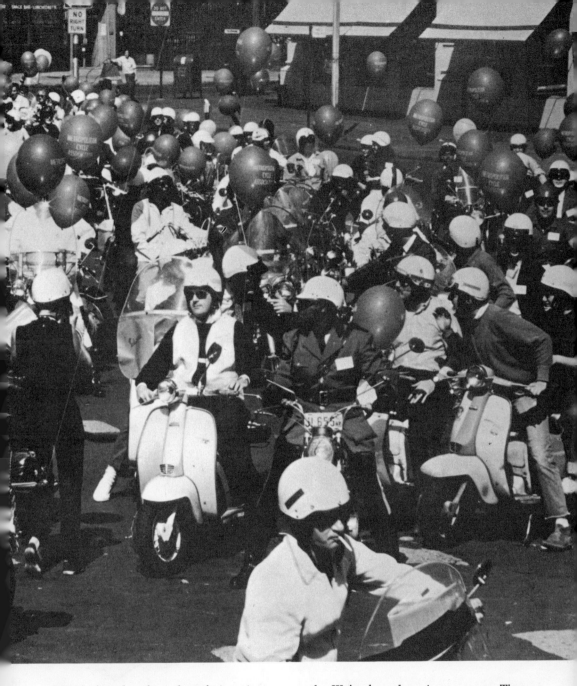

MCA's founders have lost their naivete after so much in-fighting, and now know better than to expect a simple demonstration to carry their point. What they've learned is transferable, they believe, all over the country.

"This minute we just haven't the financial capacity to do it," says Kathy Tyler of exporting their idea. "There's so much to learn. For example, nobody ever taught a motorcycle riding course before, appar-

ently. We've been learning as we go. Then there's the whole business of safety. How do you pass along all the little things you learned the hard way? Simple administrative problems—members change bikes and don't tell us. There are hundreds of things to work out. But we certainly do intend to franchise it. We can see just from the mail the kind of interest there is. Every state has these problems. We need a Triple A, we really do."

New Developments

Tire pressure, a carriage bolt and a shock cord tied to the frame hold the flexible ski on the front wheel. Track units are bolted on with passenger foot rests. Small wheels drive cleated rubber tracks.

Sidewinder

FROM TRAIL bike to snowmobile in 15 minutes is the Sidewinder's claim. An attachment that fits under-100 cc Japanese imports with unswept pipes, the Sidewinder makes 40-mile-an-hour speeds over the snow possible.

The bike's own drive chain, lengthened by a 15-inch section, drives two pairs of rubber-tired wheels off the engine sprocket. Tires in turn drive two cleated rubber tracks. An optional 12- x 40-inch ski fits on the front wheel. The Sidewinder's two drive sprockets take care of gear reduction — bike's rear-wheel sprocket acts only as an idler gear. Tracks are easily slipped off the pneumatic tires of the unit, allowing bike to be driven on ordinary roads to and from the snow fields.

Reuter, Inc., of Hopkins, Minnesota, sells its Sidewinder attachment for $248 f.o.b. factory.

Sidewinder-equipped Suzuki trail bike takes off coming over a hill top in Minnesota. Sidewinder makes 40-miles-per-hour-speeds over snow possible.

A Honda Trail 90 is commonly used with the Side winder. The motorcycle transmission, lights, horn, brakes, suspension, speedometer remain operative.

Floyd Clymer

A pair of exotic motorcycles mark pioneer Floyd Clymer's entry into manufacturing. A long-time publisher of automotive and motorcycle magazines and books, Clymer was an Indian dealer in his youth.

The Mammoth—an air-cooled, four-cylinder NSU-engined machine for the wealthy enthusiast, has a $4,000 price tag. Its overhead-camshaft mill churns out 110 hp according to its maker. With a modest 470 pounds the power-to-weight ratio is somewhat fantastic, which explains a 135 mph top speed.

Despite the relatively light weight, made possible by extensive use of magnesium-aluminum alloy, everything about the Mammoth is big. Besides its *two* headlights, the machine has a 7½-gallon gas tank, air-cooled racing-type brakes, two Weber or four Bing carburetors, electric starter, and four exhaust pipes—joined in pairs into two mufflers.

Clymer's other machine is a tribute to nostalgia, not only for Floyd himself, but for all the former Indian riders, deprived of a fresh supply, when Indian passed on in the early 1950's. The modern Indian Scout has a 45-cubic-inch side-valve V-twin engine set in a Freidle Munch frame. Indian's original bore and stroke of 2⅞ inch by 3½ inch has been retained to give the same combination of acceleration and low-end torque. (Long-stroke engines, once popular, are today unusual. Short-stroke, high-revving engines are now in favor.

The Scout is American in name only. Made in West Germany, it has Bosch electrics, Ceriani forks, and Borrani wheel rims. The frame is a slimmer version of the Mammoth's swinging-arm type. A glass fiber gas tank holds 3½ gallons; the oil tank is cast integrally with the rear fender. Rumor has it that the Scout will sell for about $1,500.

Left, two-eyed Mammoth has an air-cooled, four cylinder NSU engine originally designed for a small car. The output is 110 hp; top speed is 135 mph.

Massive front wheel on Indian Scout has racing-type brake with an air scoop for cooling. Electron casting makes bike much lighter than it looks.

Left, oil tank and saddle are built into Indian's large rear-fender casting. The fender, wheel rims, many other parts are of magnesium-aluminum alloy.

Designed especially for touring, Honda CA-175 has a single carb for smoother performance; also smaller wheels, larger fenders.

The 275 lbs. Honda 175 cc scrambler has five speeds. The dust covers on front forks and exposed springs add to sporty look.

Honda

Honda has escalated engine sizes again for 1968, with the emphasis on super-sport road bikes and scramblers. Three new displacements have made their appearance: the 125, 175 and 350 cc. There is a pair of new 125's with twin cylinder overhead-camshaft engines turning up 13 hp at 10,000 rpm. One is a super-sport road job and the other a scrambler with upswept pipes and skid plate.

A pair of 175 cc machines consists of a scrambles bike in the same trim as the 125 scrambler, and a touring road motorcycle. In the 350 cc class, the super-sport road machine and the scrambles bike pattern is repeated. Each has a surprising innovation: a five-speed transmission on the super sport and electric starting on the scrambler. The scrambler puts out 33 hp at 9,000 rpm.

Honda's 450 super sport has been slimmed and given a sleeker look. A mere 415 pounds, its top speed is said to be 115 mph. With 45 hp perking in the double-overhead camshaft twin, it covers a quarter mile in 13 seconds. A brother, the Scrambler 450, has the same power plant but a smaller gas tank, upswept exhaust pipes, and a skid plate.

Standard equipment on the new models includes turn signals, kickstands, rearview mirrors, larger tail and brake lights, rubber ball ends on clutch and brake levers, larger front brakes, and new colors—two-tones and candies.

Harley Davidson

Harley-Davidson's, and the world's, largest motorcycle continues its steady improvement. The 1968 Electra Glide has new styling touches, improved braking, a new oil pump and new air cleaner. Coupled with a 66-hp output at 5,600 rpm is an electric starter.

The 250 cc four-stroke single, the Sprint, again comes in two models. The H model has a large five-gallon gas tank, while the SS has a smaller tank and scrambling features. A limited-production 250, the CRS, is also available on special order for racing. A hotted-up Sprint engine powers a lightened machine with Ceriani forks and Pirelli competition tires.

New this year is the 125 cc Rapido two-stroke single. A high-performance piston-port engine powers a lean-looking machine with racing-style seat.

Safety is emphasized in the ultra-lightweight Harley-Davidsons. Full front and rear lighting is provided, dual-show brakes, a welded tubular steel frame, and 2.50x17 wheels with ball-bearing hubs. The 65 cc two-stroke singles come in two models: the M-65 for standard road use, and the M-65S for sportier use. Besides its racier appearance, the M-65S has a larger gas tank, by 0.9 of a gallon. Both models use the same engine.

The Harley-Davidson Electra Glide has new styling details; improved braking, oil pump and air cleaner.

The M-65 Harley-Davidson sport model is in foreground, in nearest view; standard model is at left.

Norton's new Commando has the look of a racer with its massive front brake, instrumentation and chromed fender.

All solo BMW twins will have telescopic front fork, shown at top right, instead of the once standard Earles fork.

At right is Zundapp's new 6-Day Replica, an all-out 100 cc two-stroke named for International 6-Day Trial.

BMW

When a motorcycle like the BMW—which continues for years without change—comes out with a new front fork, it's news. Beginning in the spring of 1968, all solo BMW twins will have the telescopic front fork instead of the once-standard Earles-type fork. Sidecar machines will continue to use the Earles fork because it can be adjusted for trail: reducing trail improves sidecar handling.

Norton

Norton's new Commando has the look of a racer with its massive front brake, instrumentation, chromed front fender, and saddle. A 750 cc vertical-twin engine powers an all-new machine with a frame especially designed to eliminate vibration. Weighing a mere 24 pounds, the frame has a large-diameter tube as a backbone. Swinging arm for the rear is pivoted behind the engine mounting plates. Engine is mounted in rubber to damp all possible vibrations.

Zundapp

Zundapp's 6-Day Replica is an all-out 100 cc two-stroke single competition model. Named for the International Six Days Trial in Europe, which was its proving ground, the knobby-tired lightweight has a gas-tank-mounted tool kit and a tire pump. Off-road features also include a crankcase guard and upswept exhaust pipe with perforated guard.

Motorcycle Engine Guide

AT FIRST a motorcycle seems like just a collection of odd-shaped cases, tubes, boxes, bars, cables and wires. So long as everything works there's no need to know what they call the various parts, nor how they work.

This soon changes. The first roadside breakdown and you begin to pick up pieces of nomenclature and smatterings of how the parts work. It's a disconnected education unless you read a few good motorcycle books regularly.

Sometimes attempts to learn can be more frustrating than productive. The experts often forget that not everyone is born with an instinctive knowledge of internal combustion engines. Talk of overhead camshafts, flywheels, valve tappets and the like can be intoxicating—and meaningless.

This illustrated guide, made possible by drawings from BSA, Harley-Davidson and Honda workshop manuals, is a starting point. It will help you understand how your motorcycle works, let you discuss problems with your dealer and mechanic, and add to the pleasure of reading those learned descriptions of new motorcycles in the magazines. Besides which, the machinery that makes all the fun possible is fascinating in its own right. Have a good trip. ●

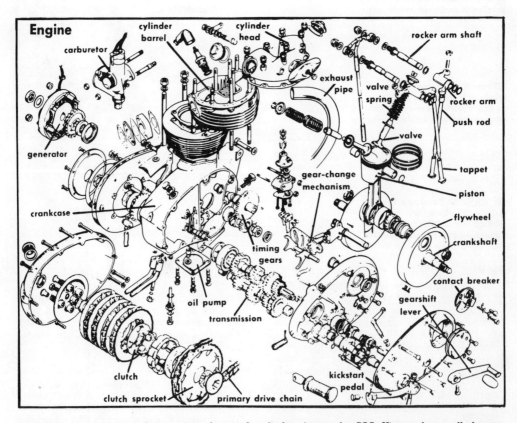

Exploded view of a complete engine, the single-cylinder, four-stroke BSA Victor, shows all the machinery it takes to convert gasoline into rear-wheel rotation. Carburetor atomizes the gas, feeds it into combustion chamber. Electricity, fed from generator to spark plug by a timing gear-driven contact breaker, explodes the gas mixture. Explosion drives piston downward and the crankshaft converts the up-and-down motion into rotary motion. The crankshaft rotation is transmitted through clutch and gearbox to rear wheel.

Carburetor

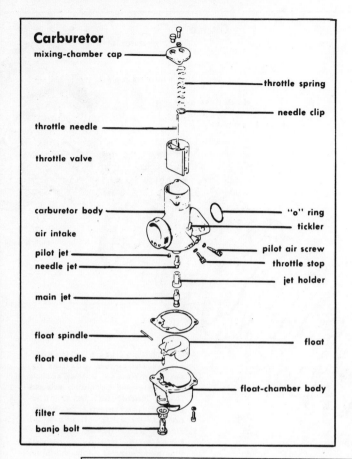

- mixing-chamber cap
- throttle spring
- needle clip
- throttle needle
- throttle valve
- carburetor body
- air intake
- "o" ring
- tickler
- pilot jet
- pilot air screw
- needle jet
- throttle stop
- jet holder
- main jet
- float spindle
- float
- float needle
- float-chamber body
- filter
- banjo bolt

Carburetors are the key to modern engines. A precise engine control at all speeds and fuel economy are the two, often conflicting, goals. In general, carburetors admit air through a hole in the side, varying the amount with a spring-loaded valve operated through a control cable from the motorcycle's handlebar twist-grip. The air, its pressure lowered by passing through a venturi (constriction), pulls gasoline from float bowl through a tiny passage or jet. Gasoline is atomized by mixing with the air and drawn into the combustion chamber when intake valve opens, exposing the carburetor to engine suction as the piston slides down in cylinder.

Alternators are common on today's motorcycles because they generate more watts than a DC generator of the same size. The slip rings of this unit used on Electra Glide are more efficient than commutator segments on armature of conventional generator.

Alternator

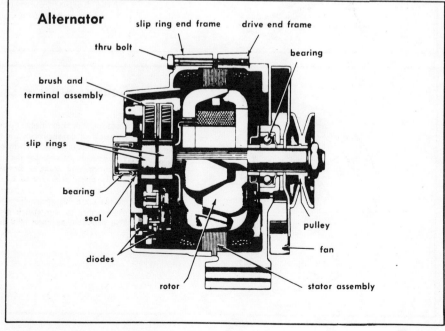

- slip ring end frame
- drive end frame
- thru bolt
- bearing
- brush and terminal assembly
- slip rings
- bearing
- seal
- diodes
- pulley
- fan
- rotor
- stator assembly

Clutch

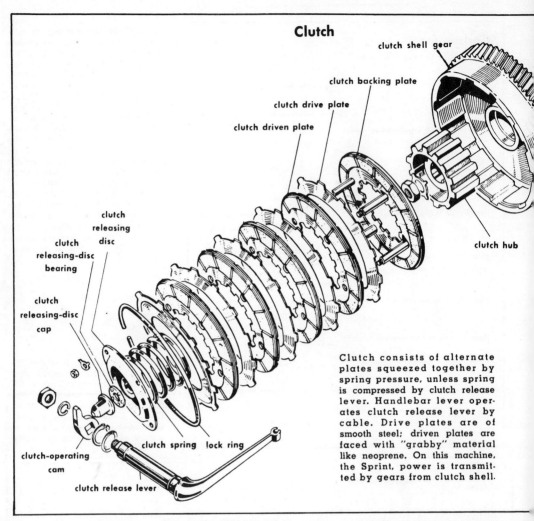

clutch shell gear

clutch backing plate

clutch drive plate

clutch driven plate

clutch hub

clutch releasing disc

clutch releasing-disc bearing

clutch releasing-disc cap

clutch-operating cam

clutch spring   lock ring

clutch release lever

Clutch consists of alternate plates squeezed together by spring pressure, unless spring is compressed by clutch release lever. Handlebar lever operates clutch release lever by cable. Drive plates are of smooth steel; driven plates are faced with "grabby" material like neoprene. On this machine, the Sprint, power is transmitted by gears from clutch shell.

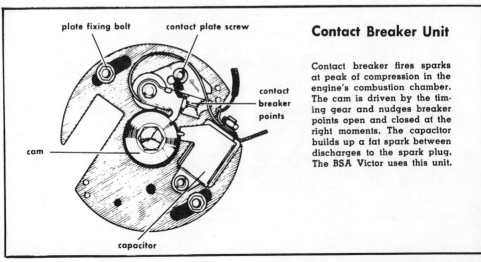

plate fixing bolt   contact plate screw

contact breaker points

cam

capacitor

Contact Breaker Unit

Contact breaker fires sparks at peak of compression in the engine's combustion chamber. The cam is driven by the timing gear and nudges breaker points open and closed at the right moments. The capacitor builds up a fat spark between discharges to the spark plug. The BSA Victor uses this unit.

Piston

Piston's up-and-down motion in cylinder barrel is transmitted through the connecting rod to the crankshaft. Left side of crankshaft on this Sprint engine, drives generator. Piston rings slip down over piston's crown and into grooves around top.

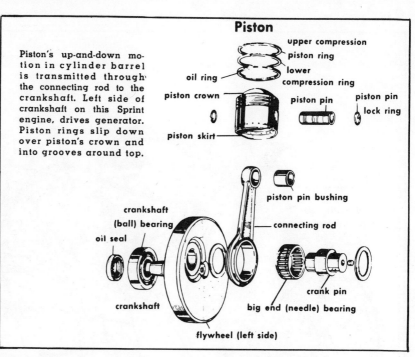

upper compression piston ring

oil ring

lower compression ring

piston crown

piston pin

piston pin lock ring

piston skirt

piston pin bushing

crankshaft (ball) bearing

connecting rod

oil seal

crankshaft

crank pin

big end (needle) bearing

flywheel (left side)

This transmission is constant-mesh type used in the Sprint. Power from clutch is transferred from main to countershaft by sliding the shifter clutches back and forth on the two shafts with shifter forks.

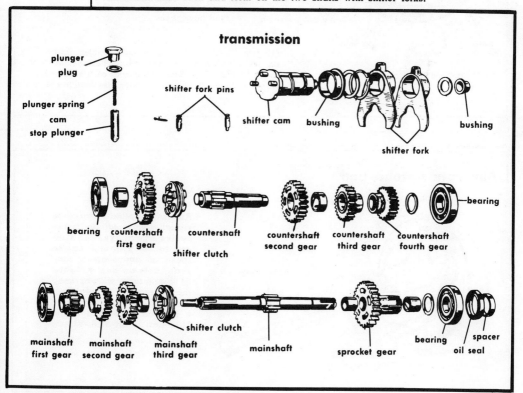

transmission

plunger plug

shifter fork pins

plunger spring cam stop plunger

shifter cam

bushing

bushing

shifter fork

bearing

bearing   countershaft first gear

countershaft shifter clutch

countershaft second gear

countershaft third gear

countershaft fourth gear

mainshaft first gear

mainshaft second gear

mainshaft third gear

shifter clutch

mainshaft

sprocket gear

bearing

spacer oil seal

Honda

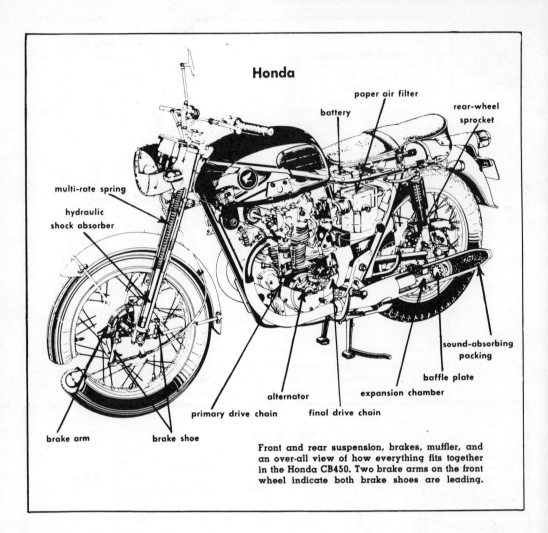

paper air filter

battery

rear-wheel sprocket

multi-rate spring

hydraulic shock absorber

sound-absorbing packing

baffle plate

expansion chamber

alternator

primary drive chain

final drive chain

brake arm

brake shoe

Front and rear suspension, brakes, muffler, and an over-all view of how everything fits together in the Honda CB450. Two brake arms on the front wheel indicate both brake shoes are leading.

Automatic Advance Unit

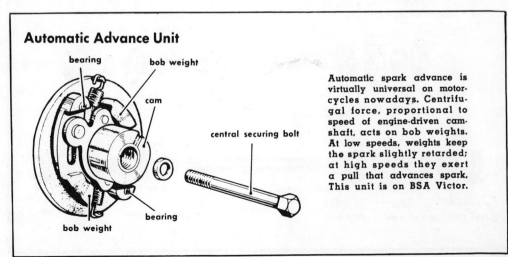

bearing

bob weight

cam

central securing bolt

bearing

bob weight

Automatic spark advance is virtually universal on motorcycles nowadays. Centrifugal force, proportional to speed of engine-driven camshaft, acts on bob weights. At low speeds, weights keep the spark slightly retarded; at high speeds they exert a pull that advances spark. This unit is on BSA Victor.

Directory

Motorcycles

Benelli (Italy)
Cosmopolitan Motors, Inc.
5521 Wayne Avenue
Philadelphia, Pa. 19144

BMW (Germany)
East — Butler & Smith, Inc.
160 West 83rd Street
New York City 10024

West — Flanders Company
200 West Walnut Street
Pasadena, Calif. 91103

BSA (England)
East — BSA Motorcycles Inc.
639 Passaic Avenue
Nutley, N. J. 17110

West — BSA Motorcycles — Western
2745 East Huntington Dr.
Duarte, Calif. 91010

Bridgestone (Japan)
Rockford Motors Inc.
1911 Harrison Avenue
Rockford, Ill. 61101

Bultaco (Spain)
Bultaco American Ltd.
2765 Scott Blvd.
Santa Clara, Calif.

Bultaco Western
11418 Burbank Blvd.
North Hollywood, Calif.

Cemoto East Importing Co.
P.O. Box 29
Schenectady, N.Y. 12301

CZ (Czechoslovakia)
East — Javco Motorcycle Corp.
38-15 Greenpoint Ave.
Long Island City, N.Y. 11101

West — Cycle Imports Inc.
1325 South LaBrea Ave.
Los Angeles, Calif. 90019

Ducati (Italy)
Berliner Motor Corporation
Hasbrouck Heights, New Jersey

Greeves (England)
Nick Nicholson Motors
11629 Vanowen
North Hollywood, Calif. 91605

Harley-Davidson (U.S.A.)
Harley-Davidson Motor Co.
Milwaukee, Wisconsin

Hodaka (Japan)
Pabatco
P.O. Box 327
Athena, Oregon 97813

Honda (Japan)
American Honda Motor Co. Inc.
Box 50
Gardena, Calif. 90247

Husqvarna (Sweden)
MED-International
P.O. Box 3571
San Diego, Calif. 92103

Jawa (Czechoslovakia)
East — Javco Motorcycle Corp.

West — Cycle Imports Inc.

Kawasaki (Japan)
East — Eastern Kawasaki Motorcycle Corp.
Avenel, New Jersey 07001

West — American Kawasaki Motorcycle Corp.
P.O. Box 2066
Gardena, Calif. 90247

Maico (Germany)
East — Gray International
4461 West Jefferson
Detroit, Michigan

West — Cooper Motors
2815 West Olive
Burbank, Calif.

Marusho (Japan)
U.S. Marusho Corp.
8588 West Washington Blvd.
Culver City, Calif. 90231

Matchless (England)
Berliner Motor Corporation

Mondial (Italy)
Chambers Enterprises
P.O. Box 20033
Long Beach, Calif. 90801

Montessa (Spain)
Montessa Motors, Inc.
3657 Beverly Boulevard
Los Angeles, Calif. 90004

Moto-Guzzi (Italy)
Premier Motor Corporation
P.O. Box 15
Leonia, N.J.

Norton (England)
Berliner Motor Corporation

Parilla (Italy)
Cosmopolitan Motors, Inc.

111

Royal Enfield (England)
Cooper Motors
2815 West Olive
Burbank, Calif.

Shillingford & Sons
1635 W. Huntington Park
Philadelphia, Pa.

Shores Motor Inc.
1981 East 8-Mile Road
Warren, Michigan

Sam Avellino
240 Harris Street
Revere, Mass.

Suzuki (Japan)
U.S. Suzuki Motor Corp.
P.O. Box 2967
Santa Fe Springs, Calif. 90670

Triumph (England)
East — The Triumph Corporation
Baltimore, Maryland 21204

West — Johnson Motors Inc.
P.O. Box 275
Duarte, Calif. 91010

Yamaha (Japan)
East — Yamaha International Corp.
One Yamaha Drive
Cherry Hill Industrial Center
Cherry Hill, N.J. 08034

West — Yamaha International Corp.
P.O. Box 54540
Los Angeles, Calif. 90054

Zundapp (Germany)
R. M. Lamb
2996 Belgium Road
Baldwinsville, N.Y.

Sidecars

Harley-Davidson (U.S.)
Harley-Davidson Motor Co.

Hollandia (Holland)
Butler & Smith, Inc.

Velorex (Czechoslovakia)
Javco Motorcycle Corp.

Watsonian (England)
R. G. Wilson
Box 54, Greendale Station
Worcester, Mass.